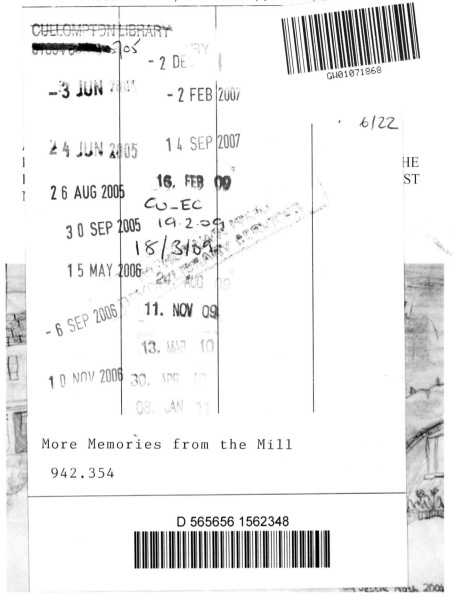

```
More Memories from the Mill

942.354
```

Painting of the Paper Mill at Hele from a photograph of the mid-nineteenth Century.
View of the Mill Yard from the Lodge.   By Jessie Nash, aged 11.   Summer 2004.

Published by Paddy Nash
Strathculm Court, Hele, Near Exeter, Devon. EX5 4PR.

ISBN 0-9540757-2-2

Printed by Short Run Press Ltd.
Bittern Road, Sowton Industrial Estate, Exeter. EX2 7LW.

Illustration of a humorous card that was attached to boxes of primroses sent by the Paper Mill in the early decades of the twentieth Century.   Similar to two other message cards in my first book 'Memories from the Mill'; page 64.

IF YOU SEEK A CALLIGRAPHIC PAGE
FOR THE KNIB OF A SENSITIVE PEN
YOU TEST THE SHEET BY SEVERAL MEANS.
WHEN SHARPLY SHAKEN IT SHOULD NOT DROOP
NOR LIMPLY SAG LIKE A SLICE OF BREAD!
INSTEAD IT CRACKLES PARCHMENT-LIKE,
CRISP AGAINST THE SLUGGISH AIR.
YOU NEED MORE PROOF? THEN LICK THE SHEET
OR RUB SOME MOISTURE IN THE PORES,
THEN IF THE OTHER SIDE STAYS DRY,
THE PAPER HAS BEEN TRULY SIZED.

Extract from Seventeenth Century poem 'Papyrus' by Father Imberdis.

View of the hill above Hele from the west of Ellerhayes.

View from the centre of Hele towards the hills to the south-east across the valley.

IV

This is the second book of individual items about Hele and the Paper Mill there; about individual people who have lived in Hele, or worked there, and about the place and the area around. As with my first collection 'Memories from the Mill' there has been research into old documents; exploration of places in the area; and again some items are recordings of people's memories; their personal thoughts. So a lot is about remembered history and that may give more than one precise account of any one time and event.

The first volume was compiled after about five years of collecting of information, recording people's memories and researching related details. Following its publication I thought to rest and follow pastures new. However I became the repository of more information, new historical artefacts and documents and most importantly more people were happy to talk to me giving me a new and extensive collection of personal memories. And all related to Hele; that small hamlet where people may erroneously think that nothing much had ever happened. How wrong they are – this second collection is full of wonderful and fascinating memories, some from people with more recent memories than those in my first book.
So once more this is not an academic study of papermaking or a chronological history, but it is amazing how the wider national and international issues interrelate and are revealed through the local issues and in individual lives; and that much has been brought to light from little-known or unrecorded facts.

I set the first book in a way to explore the reciprocal effect of the Mill, the homes and people, the social fabric and the landscape; and so hopefully whet the appetite of the reader. The response has, as I said above, been extensive so that since 2001 I have been compiling from what has come to light since then. A few facts that arose in reply to my first book and are not part of any item in this book can be recorded here. Firstly, Walter Wingrove could identify two of the men in the background of the front cover illustration of that first book. The centre man was Harold Gold and the one to the left, Bert Foan. The event was the re-starting of Machine No.1 by Mrs. Richardson in August 1934 following alterations to the machine. Secondly, there was great excitement to have shown to me a second watercolour painting of Hele by the same artist that I was able to illustrate in the first book. This second one is illustrated in this book. Also information on the man himself, who painting directly on site at houses, farms and buildings of interest; which he then sold to the owners or people locally. Finally the puzzles I had been left with in my research for the first book have to a larger extent been resolved (except that historically there is always more to hopefully discover). There are four answers in this volume on those questions I left the reader with at the end of 'Memories from the Mill'.

Once again I take sole responsibility for the content and apologise for inaccuracies. Please just enjoy this continuation of items relating to Hele and the Paper Mill.

I would like to acknowledge again with thanks all the people who have helped me this time with my second book. And especially to those people who have given their memories and contributed information to me which I have been able to use in this book.

I want to thank again the members of the Hele Conservation Society for continued support and interest.

I thank Jane Webber for proof reading and support.
I thank Stewart Penfold for computer support.

I would like to thank within the Mill, individual employees, past and present, who have been most helpful.

I have appreciated the help given by the staff of the places in which I have researched; including the local Records Office, the West Country Studies Library and the Reference Library.

Lastly, and again, I acknowledge the support of my whole family, with my grandchildren some four years older and one of them has actually used my first book from the school library for a project.

More Memories from the Mill -------
List of Contents

irlier records of Hele Mills, to the time when the grist mills
ocal farms it was then that one of the buildings at the mills
 papermaking. It would not have been at all like the later
 in buildings such as house present-day machinery. In one of
inhay or grain storage outbuildings, they would have started up
the making of sheets of paper by hand. They would have
ials, maybe grasses as well as cloth to a pulp and dipped the
 mixture and left it to drain and dry into a thin sheet of material
r.
 be talking about the middle to late eighteenth century. So
iking mill didn't create very much more of a problem of a fire
eady there with the thatched roofs and storage of hay etc. It
een of prime importance but the raw materials piled high and
acked high would have added to the risks of a fire starting and
 of product and income.
re Marks indicates the priority. The very first Fire Office in
 a firm called Phoenix in 1680 and lasted till 1711.
Fire Marks by the Royal Exchange Assurance Company which
)any:
vhich could cause the complete destruction of a man's
elihood... The fire offices came into being in order to
or losses and each office maintained their own 'fire engine

vere only in London, but then the arrangement spread across
t that anyone with a valuable property or business could pay a
 assurance company, and in the event of a fire it was seen to
trained firemen if such was needed. The alternative were that
saving property except by helpful local people using whatever
l throwing it at the blaze.
ir the fire office to issue with each policy to a new customer a
as fixed on the property to identify it to the fire engine if a fire
 such an arrangement at Hele and one was put there in 1796.
ie expenditure of a yearly premium was considered worthwhile
 business of considerable value.
)f the second design and so of an early date. The first marks
nd were die-stamped from lead about 35.5cm high and 21cm
 attractive circular design of the Royal Exchange building in
ie around the outside and a crown on the top. Those only
 s and in 1724 the second design came in and they were similar
 y still showed the building in the centre, but not the words
ey were oval in shape, with the crown on the top and had the
l, stamped at the base. They were 25cm high and 18cm wide.
 of that production.

The one at Hele was number 153796 and came under the Honiton office. The policy started from November 14th 1796 and was for a Thomas Martin, of Bradninch in the County of Devon.

Later ones varied in the use of material from lead, copper, iron, tin plate, and plain metal, with some gilded or painted. At the end of the eighteenth century the third design went into use; it was pear shaped 15.5cm high and 18cm wide with the crown removed from the top and incorporated into the main design. In 1810 they stopped having the policy number at the base due to the large increase in customers. The early 'marks', with their individual numbers, such as the Hele one have become quite a rarity. The Hele mark is no longer in place.

There could be a question as to the exact property that had this Fire Mark. The actual lead object itself is now mounted on a wooden base and stored inside safely. It had obviously been in the Hele Paper Mill's archives for some considerable time and it had been presumed to have belonged to the Mill in the past. In 1947, Mr. H.M. Richardson, the Manager at Hele for the then owners, Wiggins Teape and Co., (1919) Ltd., wrote to the Royal Exchange Assurance Company to find out about the object. They replied with all the information they had, which is given here. They all assumed the Mark had been for the paper mill at Hele. I have tried to cross link the name of Thomas Martin but cannot do so with exactitude. Thomas Martin is a name that is found as an owner and manufacturer of paper over a long and relevant period, but mostly to do with Bridge Mills (present day Silverton Mill) but possibly also at Kensham Paper Mills in Bradninch. However at the time of 1796 at Kensham, one Mill was owned by Mr. Mathews; the other by George Meach and George Rossiter.

The information of the fire mark is for a property in the parish of Bradninch and as it has ended up at Hele Mills it could be assumed there was some connection with that Mill and the ownership of the fire mark.

Details from the page of the original ledger from the Royal Exchange Assurance Office and a drawing showing the details of the item that was at Hele are illustrated on the following pages. The ledger details are copied below as the writing on the ledger page is faint.

(Policies dated 14th November)

Page no 123.   Christmas Y. 1796.

153794 Poole office;   153795 Penzance office;   153796 Honiton office;
153797 Honiton office; 153800 Edinburgh office; 153801 Edinburgh office;
(Policy Record for Thomas Martin of Hele. No. 153796 as listed above)

	Thos Martin of }	On his Dwelling House and Offices	
	Bradninch in the}	adjg. Sit. At Bradninch ofd.	100
1353796	Co. of Devon }	On a Linhay Barn, Stables and Outhouses	
50/a 3	1.6	} adjg. near of	50
100 a 5/-	5.	} All stone, Cob and Thatched	£150
2/6			

Honiton

(column of numbers below number 5.)   6.6,   9,   7.3,   8.6,   15.9,

2

Christmas 1796

Nov 14		On his Dwelling House Shop and Offices ... High Street ...	
53794			860
53796	Thos. Marling of Bradninch in the Co of Devon	On his Dwelling House and Offices adj. at Bradninch	100
		... Stables and Outhouse	50
			150
		... 1.6 / 5. / 6.6 / 7. / 8.6 / 15.9	
Hamilton	Jn Culverwell	On ... his Dwelling House	

GEORGE WEST – APPRENTICE PAPERMAKER AT HELE TO AMERICAN CONGRESSMAN

Links from the important and well-known Papermaking Family of Dewdney at Hele Mills in the nineteenth century can be followed through an apprentice that learnt the skills of the trade before emigrating and making good in America with family links still in the paper industry.

George West, the father of the apprentice George, was born in Frome in Somerset. He and his wife and family moved to Devon. It is assumed that he was an agricultural worker and moved from farm to farm as so many men did in the early nineteenth century. They had a large family with one son born in Kentisbeare in 1823 and he was called George after his father. Shortly afterwards they moved to Bradninch and stayed, because they were still there when at the age of between ten and twelve years he started work at one of the two Paper-Mills at Kensham. Those mills were on the river Culm, at the bottom of Kensham Avenue after going down Mill Way from the town centre.

Young George then went to Hele Mill when he was fourteen, apprenticed under the owner, the renowned paper manufacturer, Mr. Dewdney. He learnt all the skills, and by the age of twenty-one was in charge of the metal-works shop.

George stayed in Bradninch and at Hele Mill until he was thirty-one or two when in 1854/5 he emigrated to America with his wife and children. They had six children but very sadly when they arrived in America the youngest daughter of that time died. He also took with him his father, and a sister. They all three appeared on an American census of 1855. Sadly, his mother, Jane, had died in that year of 1854, and maybe that event opened up the possibility of the move across the Atlantic and was the reason why he took his father, an old man, on that venture. George, the paper-maker made his way and prospered in the New World. It is simplest to quote from Croslegh's 'History of Bradninch', written early in the twentieth century:

'...he pursued the business to which he had been brought up, and with such success that in process of time he found himself the owner of seven paper mills, throwing out each day twenty-seven tons of paper, and also of a large paper-bag factory, which produced 200,000,000 bags a year. His energy, however, overflowed into other channels, such as the building of railways and other enterprises. He became president of the first national bank at Balston Spar, in the state of New York; and in 1880 he was elected a member of the house of representatives for the 20th New York District, being looked upon as one of the most wealthy and influential members of congress.'

At the age of fifty-one, twenty years after his arrival there in America, he had not forgotten his mother, left behind in the grave-yard in Bradninch. He arranged for a beautiful stained-glass window to be installed in the Ladies Chapel of St. Disens Church, the Parish Church of Bradninch. The large complex fully stained-glass design was installed at his own expense. A brass plaque with fine lettering was fixed next to it to commemorate his mother. It is not known if he himself returned personally to instruct this memorial. There may have been members of the family who still lived in Bradninch, who could have carried out the commission for him. The grave of Jane is in the Church grave-yard directly in front of the East (Altar) end. The headstone is of plain grey stone with a half-circular top and is only slightly weathered. The inscription on it is:

Sacred to the memory of JANE wife of GEORGE WEST Who died 14 APRIL 1854 Aged 61 years. This stone is erected by her son The Hon. GEORGE WEST of Balston Saratogh Co. New York.

To really consider George and think about how he came to be so successful after he emigrated one needs to look at the time he spent at Hele Mill. He had spent about two years at Kensham Mill as a boy. John Dewdney owned Hele Mill but of course the Mill Owners knew each other and would have known about the people employed under them. To become a Papermaker was high status and took years of apprenticeship. It was not easy to get apprenticed; some boys taken on continued in lower skilled work or as labourers. George must have stood out from the crowd and shown aptitude for Dewdney to take him from the other Mill, especially as sons from his own workforce would usually have had preference.

The Dewdney papermaking family was very experienced. The generations running it at Hele from before 1837 had developed many innovations. After a disastrous fire in 1821 rebuilding provided a modern structure. The old waterwheel was replaced by a water turbine and steam power ran a new paper machine; gas was put into the building for lighting so it can be seen that Dewdney was aware of and took on the latest industrial processes. The move from individual hand-made sheets of paper to continuous rolls of paper was a major move forward and opened up opportunities for progress and gain. They had also found a supply of spring water nearby that allowed them to produce better paper than from that produced using the river water. So for George being there as an apprentice, he had an inventive and positive management and workforce to learn from.

This was also the era of even greater innovation and success. To start with, Dewdney invented the process of smoothing or 'glazing' the writing paper to produce a very superior product that was much sought after. Hele was at the forefront of the paper making in England. It provided the paper for the catalogue of the Prince Albert Great Exhibition in London of 1851 and also won gold medals in it for other papers produced. George had become an important member of the work force as he was in charge of the metal-works shop at the age of twenty-one in about 1844 and so he must have been involved in this activity and learnt from it.

At Hele another step forward was the laying of the London to Exeter, via Bristol, Railway by Brunel. It passed through Hele with a station and sidings just next to the Mill. The far-seeing Dewdney achieved ease of receiving deliveries of his materials and dispersal of his products through this new communication network. Dewdney may have had some effective influence to have the line laid so close to his Mill on its course through that part of Devon. It proved more efficient in the long run to use the railway rather than the old methods of horse and cart to the local Port of Topsham some ten miles away involving loading on barges etc for transport to other ports in the country. The railway was opened in May 1844 so George would have watched its construction and been there to see it in operation before he left ten years later.

On a very different level, but of probably equal importance George would have seen Dewdney build a village right in Hele, close to the Mill for the more important members of his workforce. They were well thought-out homes and the Square of houses included a Chapel and later a Post Office. Also, the earlier Thomas Dewdney had shown the same concerns for well-being of the workers. In his will following his death in 1827 he left a sum of money to be invested by the Mayor and Burgesses of Bradninch:

'for ever the sum of fifty pounds upon trust to lay out ..bread to the poor..'

John Dewdney sold the business in 1852 and retired to Starcross on the Exe estuary. The new owner Charles Collins, the son-in law of William Johnson, who was of another famous papermaking family continued the improvements and alterations of production. The following year one of the finest papermaking machines in England was installed at Hele and they stopped doing the older process of hand-made paper.

Why George emigrated is an interesting question. The opportunities may have seemed compelling to a hard-working highly skilled craftsman. He may have liked working under Dewdney; he may have not got on with Collins the new owner. He may have seen a better future for himself as a fairly young man with a young family; to leave quiet Devon and take all the risks of crossing the Atlantic in the mid-nineteenth century for the possibility of prospects of money and fame in the New World. His mother's death seems to be linked, either he didn't want to leave while she was alive; or maybe she would not cross the Atlantic or maybe she became ill and he remained until she died. There could be both family and employment issues that spurred him to just that precise time of leaving. Maybe the family records of later generations in America had the answer in them.

In America he made good use of his experience in Hele. He was the first to produce watermarked paper and glazed paper in America and both of these innovations were produced at Hele at the time when George West was there. When he died he was worth three million dollars, which was some fortune in those days, and reflects hard work and some creative entrepreneurial skills. He lived a long life to about 78 years, with his wife dying in the same year. By all accounts he led a religious, goodly life as a benefactor as well as a businessman.

The Censuses for Bradninch during the nineteenth century give some information on George West's family. He lived in Bradninch from about 1824 to 1854. The earliest Censuses of 1841 and 1851 cover that time but there was leaway to the nearest five years on the exact age for adults and also parts are difficult to read in detail. George was in the Census of 1841, in a house in Fore Street. His mother, Jane West, aged 45, was Head of house; maybe his father was away at that time. She and daughters, Susanna aged 20 and Martha aged 15 were all Paper Packers in a Mill. Sons, Henry aged 20 and George (our man) aged 18 were Papermakers. Also of the household was the younger daughter, Louisa aged 1; and Mary Ann Wilson aged 25 and Ann Mardon aged 20, both were Paper Packers. Lastly, Charlotte Hilt aged 2.

The Census of 1851 revealed a different West household. It was again in Fore Street, three dwellings down from the Castle Inn, which was next to the Guildhall. George West aged 72, and wife, Jane, were on their own. He was born in Frome so was George's father and classified as a Papermaker Pauper, meaning he had no means of support; while Jane was by then an Overlooker at Papermill. The Census tells us she was born in Bradninch, which explains why the family had settled in the town after several moves around Devon.

Of interest to George's future were two households, also in Fore Street. In one house in the 1841 Census was Richard Rose aged 40, and his wife, Mary, aged 45, and children, Mary 15; Richard 14; Henry 12; and Emma 4; He was a Papermaker. Two houses from them was the household of John Baker aged 45, with his wife, Elizabeth, aged 40, and four children aged 9 months to 12 years. He was an Agricultural Labourer. Also John Rose, aged 70, as a Papermaker and Louise Rose aged 18, as a Paper Roller. It would seem that Louise as the eldest child of Richard and Mary Rose had left home and John Rose was most likely her grandfather. There is a fine gravestone close to the Parish Church, to an earlier Rose and his wife, Ann, dated about 1836, but it is too weathered to identify exactly.

George was married to Louise Rose on the 4th April 1844 in Bradninch. After the emigration to America other persons of the name West continued in Bradninch, appearing on the 1861 Census until the 1891 Census. They may link to our George West family.

Francis West was born in 1820 in Doddicombe in Devon and could have been the eldest brother. In 1861 he, with wife Ann and children, Elizabeth, George and Joseph lived in West End Road adjoining the large house Dunmore. Francis was a servant and it could be that following his father's occupation he worked in some agricultural position for William H Besly of Dunmore, who was also Mayor of Bradninch. William and George, the two younger brothers, probably went into Papermaking as they were brought up in a town that had that industry.

In 1871 Francis West and his family lived in Parsonage Street and he was now identified as being employed as a Domestic Coachman. The children were all still at home with Elizabeth aged 15 as a Laundress, George aged 14 working in the Paper Mill, Joseph aged 12 still a Scholar and Prescilla, Ann, Margaret and Betha all younger and at home.

In 1881 the only household in Bradninch to have occupants named West, this time in Beacon Road, was of George West, the son; now 24 with a wife Emma and a daughter of a few months old. He was a Papermaker at Hele Mill and his wife a dressmaker.

In 1891 there was only Joseph West, the second son of Francis. He was then 32, with wife Mary, and children Francis, Wilfred and Annie. They lived in Fore Street and he was a Papermaker. . There are quite a few links in names and occupations to the past, if they were of the same family as our George West.

On the following page are illustrations of the Stained-glass Window and Plaque in Bradninch Parish Church, St Disen; dedicated to Jane West, mother of George West.

My thanks to Rosemary Lowe, Church Street, Bradninch for introduction to the relevance of George West in Bradninch. She and George West's descendants have extra information on the family history in American.

The plaque about 18"x 12" has a religious design on the left-hand side, the lettering is in Gothic script with black in-fill and red in-fill in the main letters. It was made by John Hardman & Co. Birmm.   The inscription is as follows:

> TO THE GLORY OF GOD & TO THE DEAR
> MEMORY OF JANE WEST, WHO DIED 14th
> APRIL, A D 1854, THIS WINDOW IS
> ERECTED BY HER SON, THE HON: GEORGE
> WEST, MEMBER OF CONGRESS, U S.

THE WATER MARK OF JOHN DEWDNEY 1849 – ON DANDY ROLL AND MOULD

We have back here in Hele two very special artefacts that have survived to the twenty-first century; having been kept, with care, in storage for 150 years.
One is a sieve mould that was used to make hand-made sheets of paper and the other is a short length of a Dandy Roll that was put into the paper machine, which produced continuous paper. Both of these items have the wire watermark image welded onto the wire mesh.

That watermark is of the words 'JOHN DEWDNEY 1849' below an image of Britannia in an oval disc topped with a crown.

The mould that was used for making single sheets of hand-made paper is made of a wooden frame, 460mm x 380mm, with 17 thin wooden strips slotted between the longer sides, kept spaced apart by a central metal rod. It is covered on the front by a sheet of very fine metal mesh fixed on all the frame edges by metal strips held in with small metal pins hammered flat. There are slightly thicker strands of wire fixed on top of the mesh between the longer sides that keep the fine mesh equally spaced. The metal image already described, just one, is exactly in the centre, with the Britannia image on the left and the name on the right with the date immediately beneath.

The length of dandy roll is a section cut from a roll that would have been the width of the paper machine. This artefact is of the same wire mesh with the same slightly thicker wires to hold the mesh in place, again 460mm long but now rolled round with wooden ends of 100mm dia. and a metal strip along its length to hold it in place. It has a central rod that fixed it into place on the machine. This has exactly the same metal image as already described and is in the same position as on the mould. The pulp that at that stage was thin 'wet-paper' passed against this roller and the metal image of the 'watermark' being on top of the supporting mesh would press into it and so create thinner paper at that point. Later, when the paper is held up to the light, the subtle image appears.   Similarly, with the hand made paper in the mould, the metal image that becomes the 'watermark' is on top of the flat mesh and so the layer of pulp that dries out to become paper ends up thinner at that point. Again, later, when held up to the light the image is seen.

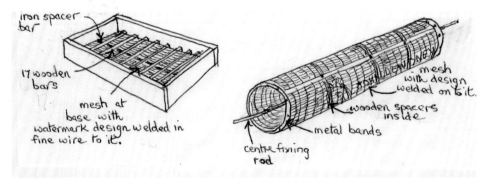

Previous information on the Dewdney Family is in an item 'The Dewdney family at Hele' in my first book, 'Memories from the Mill', page 9.

Illustration of the metal watermark designed at the Hele Paper Mill in 1849.

THE VISIT OF THE PRINCE OF WALES TO HELE MILLS IN 1921.

The paper mill at Hele had, since 1767, always been run as a family business. It had changed hands from one individual to another in varying circumstances but always bought or taken over by a practical resident papermaker and manufacturer. It became The Hele Paper Company in 1892 but was still owned and run by the family members of the previous owner. In 1920 the Company was bought by Wiggins Teape Ltd. They, in comparison to the Hele Paper Company, were a large, well-established and successful papermaking firm owning mills in various parts of England. And so the paper mill in Hele finally became part of a wider industrial system.

A year after this ownership there was a visit from the then Prince of Wales, Prince Edward, who later became king for such a short while in 1936 before abdicating. No detailed written information within the mill records of the event have been found but there are some fascinating photographs of his visit, seven of which are shown on the following pages.

The first one, on previous page, is of the arrival of H R H the Prince of Wales and his greeting the management and family members outside the Mill House Offices in the Mill yard. Mr. Patrick Hepburn, a member of the former family owners was Managing Director of Wiggins Teape and was the guide around the Mill.

The second is of the first work-shop in the Mill itself and the early process of papermaking. It is in the Rag Room where the women were ripping up second hand cloth into small strips which were then put into boilers to be broken down to become part of the raw material to be turned into paper.

The third illustration is of the Prince as he visited the Beater Room, where he was shown the large vats of liquid pulp by Mr. Hepburn.

The fourth illustration is of the Prince studying the paper-making machine as the process was being explained to him. The Machine room is seen here as being at that time a complicated and difficult environment.

The fifth illustration is of the finishing end of the paper-making machine and shows the paper that was produced ending as a large roll.

The sixth illustration again shows the Prince and Mr.Hepburn, this time studying the finished paper cut into sheets.

The seventh and final illustration is of the final phase of the visit with the Prince sitting in his fine limousine with Mr. Hepburn and Mr. Horsburgh of the Mill saying goodbye. This is on page 20.

On the page after the fifth and sixth illustrations, page 17, is illustrated the Prince of Wales's signature in the Visitors Book of the Mill. It is on the left-hand page on its own – 'Edward R' – but with the heading Whit Tuesday 17th May 1921. The visit is known to have been on the 21st June 1921. Presumably having headed that page in May it was not used until the Royal visit. The right-hand page following has the signatures of the five people accompanying the Prince.

On the back cover of this book is an illustration of the Prince of Wales signing the Visitors Book on this visit.

A separate item on the Visitors Book is on page 84.

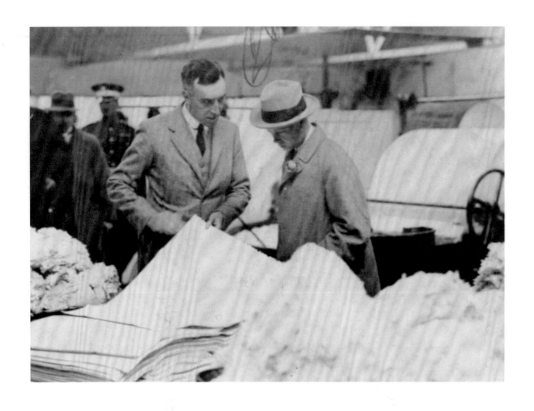

DATE · · · · · · · · NAME · · · · · · · · ADDRESS

Whit Tuesday   17ᵗʰ May 1921.

[signatures]

17

THE LAYOUT OF THE MILL – DEVON VALLEY MILL IN 1925.

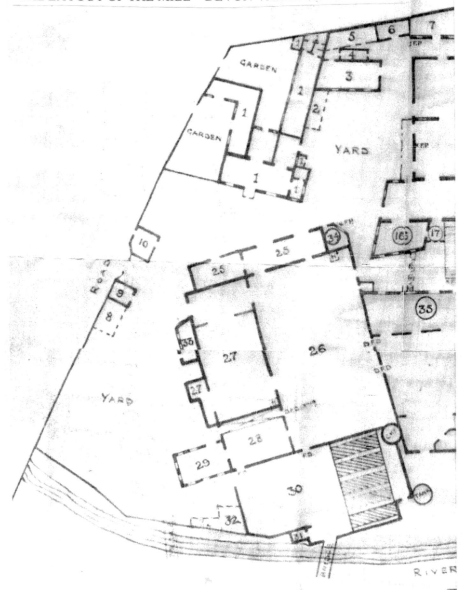

List of buildings: Offices 1; Oil Store 2; Carpenters Shop 3; Paint Shop 3,4; Fodder
Store 6; Store 7; Store & Cycle Shed 8; Fire Engine House 9; Time Office 10; Store &
Dusting 11; Dust Chamber 12; Stores 13; Stores, Dusting & Rag Boiling 14–22; Filter
Houses 23,24; Beater Houses, Stores & Engine House 25–29; Boiler House 30,31; Stores
32; Dynamo House 33; Pump House 34; Machine Room & Salle 35–39,41–43,
45,46;Cutting, Tub Sizing & Boiling 44, 47–52; Stockrooms 53;

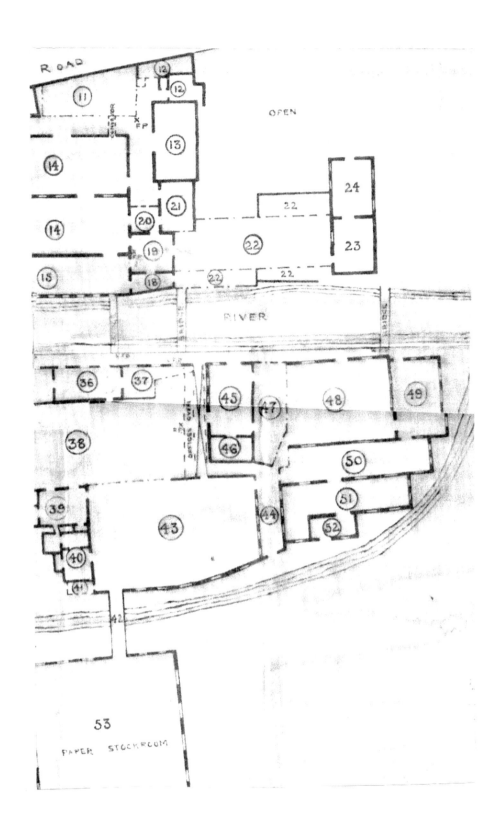

ROAD

OPEN

RIVER

53

PAPER STOCKROOM

THE LAYOUT OF THE MILL – DEVON VALLEY MILL IN 1925.

On the previous two pages is the layout of Mill buildings in 1925. This has come to light since I produced my first book 'Memories from the Mill' in which I showed the layout map of the Mill buildings in 1848. I am pleased to produce this layout as it complements the earlier one and comparisons made as to the expansion of the Mill during the intervening 75 years. This plan has a few interesting items. The whole entrance into the Mill complex was no longer on Hele Road opposite Hilly Lane. The dwelling house remained the same with smaller gardens attached, and the main entrance was off Station Road through gates into the Mill Yard that had been the larger part of the garden. The Time Office was on one side of the gates, which is known as The Lodge today and interestingly on the other side was the Fire Engine House. From information in a separate item on the early Fire Mark and fire hazards it seems as if they kept fire-fighting equipment on the premises in 1925. The Mill was very compact in its layout with the leat going, as now, into the Mill from the upstream of the river with only the Storerooms over the River Culm itself.

That area identified as open was in earlier times the gardens of Venmans, the very old house, just next to it along Hele Road. Today nissen style buildings are there, used as workshops and offices. Since the 1950's there has been expansions of the workshops, Boiler house and Machine Rooms, especially for the larger papermaking machines in use; and some of that expansion has taken place on the other side of the river.

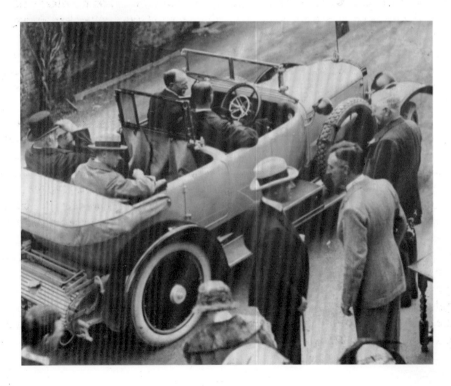

A FAMILY OF CULLOMPTON HILL – MEMORIES OF VIOLET BROOM.

I was born in the early months of 1921. I left school at the age of fourteen at the end of the Easter term as it followed on from my birthday. My best friend had been able to leave at Christmas time as her birthday had been in the Autumn and at the time I envied her. I went to the Bradninch Infants and Junior School, which had been at the Old School behind the Guildhall. Then I went on to the Girl's School in West End Road; this was just before the Garage and was brick-built and is now the Scout Hall.

I didn't go to Cullompton although there was a larger Girl's School there as there was difficulty getting there. That one, now demolished, had been on the site that is now the Health Centre and Magistrates Court at this end of the Fore Street. The difficulty for us in Bradninch in the nineteen-thirties was that there was not a regular bus service. If we went by train we would have had to walk to Hele Station, going a mile and a half in the opposite direction, and then a long walk from Cullompton Station which was well out to the further side of the town, right back through the town to this end of Fore street. We did have to go from our School in Bradninch to that school in Cullompton a few times to learn cooking. Those visits were quite an event as we had to walk the three miles there and back and it took up most of the day; but sometimes, luckily, we would be given a lift if a vehicle was passing us as we walked.

I have lived on Cullompton Hill as far as I can remember all my life; with moving into No.13 when I was seven, where I am still. Mother and Father lived in Bradninch before this in one of the cottages lower down the hill on the other side. Father had been born in Bradninch and Grandfather and Grandmother had always lived in one of the centre houses in the row below No.13 on the same side. My mother was not local; that is she did not come from a Bradninch family. She was Eva Brookes before she married father and came from Cullompton. For us when I was young, and for the generations before me, Cullompton was not local – it was far off and was more of an event to visit there.

It was an interesting area on Cullompton Hill. It was very steep with walls at the bottom and very little space for a footpath when they came later to put one in. Our house was very near the top, in fact the ground at the back could not be cultivated it was just too steep and is covered in shrub and brambles right from the back wall. It sits connected to another cottage by a side passage and they sit sideways to the road built along the slope of the hill and not up it like the lower ones are. We used to have the front door facing and close out to the road with a few steep steps direct to the roadway. That has long been blocked up and the front door goes out to the garden in front of us and then along a path and steps to the road. This is safer now, but the traffic today is very fast going past, and noisy; it was much quieter when I was young and safe as there were mainly horses and carts and only a few buses struggling up the hill.

On the other side of the hill opposite us there was a row of cottages, three I think as far as I recall and they lay alongside to the road. I think one person was the landlord of all the houses on Cullompton Hill. One of the row on the other side fell down, they were in a poor condition and not well looked after; the people in all of them were re-housed by the Council and then they were all pulled down and not rebuilt.

That land became another steep slope to the top of the hill covered in scrubby trees and brambles until a few years ago. Then they built a whole estate of houses, called Heggedon Close, on the land on that side of the road including up to where the row of cottages had been. So people live on the hill there again.

I started work at Hele Mill as soon as I had left school. The Mill employed a lot of women then in several departments, not as now, the situation is not similar. I was a Sorter when taken on, the men brought the paper in from the cutting-room to the Salle; that was the finishing-room. The paper was dragged in on a wooden trolley which had been made of scaffold poles joined together. This was loaded with the paper already cut to size. On the benches two girls worked one each side of a block of paper and sorted through, throwing aside damaged sheets. The good was moved over the back onto another bench. Further into the room were the Counters; these were girls who sat and counted the sheets into numbered piles depending on the size and weight – so many were piled up to get a certain quantity such as a half ream or ream etc. The ream or half ream was the term for certain weights so that with thinner paper there were more sheets.

The two Sorters to each block of paper fed one Counter and when she called for it we would take a pile of paper to her. It was carried over the arm and shoulder to her except for the largest size paper which was too big and heavy to carry that way and had to be carried flat. Some of the time while I worked in the Salle there was piece-rate paid on how many reams we had supplied. The Counter put a label assigning it on the reams after counting and sent the information up to the Office. There was one order for blotting-paper for Vernons Football Pools that gave us good money for a few weeks. They required extra-large sheets but thinner than usual and two sorters had to work together handling it and we could work it quite quickly together. Later this system was stopped and all got paid a day rate.

The normal paper we worked with was in the three small sizes; large post as the smallest, then medium, then double cap. Twice the size of each of those were double in front, double and quad.

There was always blotting-paper produced, and it was always folded over in four or six sheets together. A wooden block was used to press the join down; there were then ten lots of the six sheets to a half ream and it was sometimes glued at the fold into a block. It was made in all colours, and ordinary paper also came in all colours with names to them such as azure, sky blue, pale pink, cirrus (dark pink), light and dark green, canary yellow, dark blue, cream, etc. and several shades of grey.

The girls and women worked well together and supported each other, especially individual friends and those that fitted in together. There were girls who moved over to labelling with several labels to stick onto the packed reams of paper. A top one was blue, a bottom one white; then another girl put a side label on to say it was made in Great Britain. The Mill had customers from all over the world. At first

22

the wrapped-up reams were taped up, not tied. The glue was made in the Blacksmith Department, I think from animal bones, but we had it as granules and mixed it with water and it was very runny and messy as the girls had to brush it on to strips of paper before putting that around the package. Later the glue improved and was better to use, it was like Gloy, which you could buy in the shops. Then we used cello-tape and had tape-machines.

I worked all my life at Hele, except for wartime between 1939 to 1945. I retired when I was sixty. Grandfather had worked all his life as far as I know at Silverton Mill on the paper machines. He always either walked or used a bike each day to work, it being about a mile or so on past Hele. Father followed him in Silverton Mill and did several different jobs to do with papermaking. At the outbreak of war I was eighteen and had to sign up. I went into Munitions. I went to Bristol for training, two other girls from the Salle went also. I worked in Bristol afterwards and was in lodgings. One of the others went to Chard and one to somewhere in Wiltshire. It was all organised like being in the forces. Luckily for me it was arranged for my pension payments to be carried through the war so when I returned to Hele and carried on till my retirement without a break I had a full pension for all my years.

When I started again at Hele after the war Mr. Frank Tett was foreman in charge of the Salle, but he retired in 1956 as Finishing Manager, and then Mrs. Maddock was the Supervisor. I have a photograph of all of us who were working in the Salle in 1952, and she is sitting central in the front row, and I am on the back row second in from the right. There were forty-one ladies of the Salle, which shows the large number of people needed to work the finishing and packing of the paper. Mrs Amy Davey followed on as Supervisor. I became an Inspectress. This meant I had to take out paper from each Sorter and check that they hadn't left too many poor sheets in the pile. If there were too many they had to sort it all again. Violet Titley was the other Inspectress and went on to be the Dispatch Clerk. I was presented with a gold watch by Wiggins Teape in 1974 at the Rougemont Hotel in Exeter for thirty-nine years unbroken service. I had already had a gift for fifteen years service; we had a choice then of a small silver dish, a pen and pencil set or a large cut-glass bowl which is what I chose and have still on the sideboard.

Going back to earlier times, after the improvement to the packing and labelling of the reams, they brought in a counting machine to replace the girls counting but it was not good. It was always going wrong. They put men to work it and it was alright if they were steady and careful but they were often wanting to do it too quickly for the machine to cope with. The machine had been made I think in the Blacksmith Shop, they seemed to produce items that were needed rather than buy something in. There was a cutting-room next to the Salle that the paper went to prior to us. It had two guillotines with two men working each one cutting it off the roll that came off the paper-machine. After the counting of the paper it went back to be finally trimmed to correct size before being wrapped. The guillotine machines were worked on three shifts continuously which goes to show how much paper went through.

Because the paper had been cut on the guillotine prior to the sorting the edge of the paper often cut the hands and fingers. We used to have boxes of sticky plasters and cover the cuts. One girl was allergic to the plasters and took her own plasters in but sometimes she and another one used the sticky tape that we used to tape up the reams of paper into parcels. As I've said this was very sticky glue and their hands were covered in this brown tape at times but it worked for them and somehow they managed to sort the sheets. We wore our own clothes at work but were given lengths of felt canvas to lay across the lap to protect them. Later we had nice overalls, rather pretty pink check pattern to wear at work.

When the Rag Room closed down when the Mill went over to using all wood pulp, the girls there came over to work with us. Over time however fewer girls were needed as more of the tasks were done mechanically, and more customers bought paper in bulk rolls and cut it themselves. They might have sometimes wanted to print on it first if it was for a special purpose. Anyway it did mean that as people left they were not always replaced and in the end, but after I had retired, there was only one woman left to work in the Salle from the old days and she was given odd jobs to do until she retired. When I started there were six girls on sorting; nine on counting and three on pasting labels.

My family was always in Bradninch and seemed to me to have been in paper making work. I think though that thinking of today there is a special link between my family and paper-making. I had one brother younger than me and at secondary age he went to Tiverton School. He joined the R.A.F. with two other boys and was an apprentice for accountancy, and he went to many parts of the world. This was a break from the close-knit family on Cullompton Hill as he didn't return to live there and married a girl from the Midlands. He had a daughter and son and he, my nephew, has gone to South Africa to work. He was trained as an engineer and will most likely stay. He likes the climate and now has his own family growing up there. My younger days revolved around family life, and now I am very fond of the family of my brother, especially as I never married.

The link of my nephew back to Hele Mills comes through paper. The Mill sold paper to South Africa in the past, probably to the Government for official paperwork. It used to have a watermark set into it as it was produced which was a design of the national flower emblem. My nephew has recently sent me a china ornament that is of the flower that is used as the South African emblem and this reminds me so much of that watermarked paper. The flower is named King Protea, I hope that is its correct name, it has cactus-like leaves in a circle around a big solid flower centre.

Although I have never ventured far but lived all my life here in this house with my parents, I enjoyed my younger days in Bradninch. I used to love best to go to the cinema in Cullompton most Saturday afternoons but just occasionally an extra visit during the week as small buses, like a coach, had started to go to Cullompton from Bradninch. The cinema was in the large Bullring where the carpet shop is now. I also liked to go into Exeter to look at the shops and to go to the pictures there. There was a sixpenny return train ticket from the Hele Station on Thursdays at six-thirty and I sometimes went on that after work. The trains ran often and late into the evening so I was able to go to the pictures and in season to the Pantomime which I enjoyed.

There were many social activities from the Mill. There were outings by coach to such places as Torquay, Paignton etc. We would have a coffee stop at a hotel on the way, lunch at another hotel which had been booked for us; then we were free to look at the town and the shops which I liked. We were given money for our tea which we could have wherever we liked and then returned in the evening. There were lots of those visits and I continued going on them after I retired; there were also lunch events in my retirement in the Mill canteen. The canteen was always good at providing meals. One visit of our retirement group was arranged by George Cunnings in that we went down to the Ivybridge Mill near Plymouth. George Cunnings had originally come to Hele from a Mill called Stoneywood in Scotland and his son had been at Hele but went on to be Manager at Ivybridge. Some of us after lunch were able to go into Plymouth to look at the shops in place of the guided tour of the Mill, and I did that as I felt I knew enough about papermaking and Plymouth was further than I would go normally.

The Mill at Hele had a lot of sporting events. It had a very strong running group as well as athletics, tug-of-war, football and cricket teams. Some of the teams went away for weekend to compete against other mills as far away as Hampshire.

The only time I didn't go to work was when there were floods at Hele. One time it went right through the Mill and the Salle, so I was sent home, and another time a man came up to Bradninch to stop us going down as it was so flooded, so I went back home for the day. On such days it would flood right into Hele Square and the houses there including Katie Andress's Post Office. The only other time I was not at work was when I had to stay home for a while to care for my mother.

Now I go to the Gospel Hall women's group on Wednesday evenings and Sundays. When a child and young the family went to the Baptist Church in town and which had events in the hall behind the Church, such as music, concerts, prize-giving and other events linked to the Church. I belonged to the Baptist Christian Endeavour Group. I was happy with those links to Church and with family and friends close at hand.

National Floral Symbol of the Republic of South Africa. Protea cynaroide.

The Giant King Protea is one of the most widespread of the Cape proteas. The early collectors referred to the artichoke like flower heads of the King Protea. The name hardly does justice to the magnificent heads which are the largest in the genus. Variations in colour include the beautiful pale silvery-pink flower bracts.

Illustration from a 1952 Photograph of the Salle Ladies. Violet is standing on the back row, second from the right, Mrs.Maddock, the Supervisor, is in the front row, fourth from the right.

Violet worked in Hele Mills during the twentieth century at a time when there was great achievement in paper production. Wiggin Teape Ltd was a very astute business but also was strong on its care and involvement with the well being of its workforce. The result was a workforce loyal and long serving as the following document shows.

Devon Valley Mill -- Presentation of Long Service Awards, 21st October, 1974.

...........WIGGINS TEAPE are a major international group of Papermakers, operating 13 Paper Mills and 7 Factories in Britain; Paper Mills in Belgium, India and Brazil; Factories in Eire, South Africa, Nigeria, Kenya and Zambia; together with substantial interests in Paper Mills in Australia and Argentina. The Queen's Award to Industry has been awarded to the Company on three separate occasions, twice for export achievement and earlier this year for technological innovation. At the Devon Valley Mill, Hele, Nr. Exeter, the majority of production consists of specialised papers for industrial use – papers used in the manufacture of plastics laminates, Fuel and air filter elements for the motor vehicles, wet-acid battery separators also, besides which writing, printing and blotting papers are produced.

Besides a financial award payable on retirement, employees are now presented with awards after 15 years and after 35 years. The thirty employees who received gold watches [for the longer term] were 8 members of staff and 22 production and maintenance workers. ...... Between them they have given 1251 years of service to the Company, an average of nearly 42 years each. The longest serving recipient was Mr. Percy Budd of Cullompton who had worked at the Mill for more than 50 years and who will retire in May of next year. His family can claim a good record of service. His father, an older brother, and four sisters have all been employed in past years and two other brothers and a grand-daughter are still on the payroll. Two sets of brothers, Mr. Roy Norman (Head Papermaker) and Mr. Ron Norman (Maintenance Fitter) with Mr. Reg. Gitsham (Head Stoker) and Mr. Leonard Gitsham (Guillotine Man) were among those receiving watches.

.... The Mill Manager, Mr. J.Burnett, in commenting on the valuable and loyal service records, challenged the Press to find another Company in the area employing more than 200 who could better the achievement of more than 12% of their total number with 35 years or more of completed and unbroken service. Later in the year 87 employees, constituting more than a third of the workforce at the Mill, will receive awards for 15 years service.

This statement was written by Mr. Rodney Goff, Personnel Services Manager at that time.

Violet Broom is listed as completing 39 years and retiring as an Inspectress.

The list of recipients has been recorded in the first book 'Memories from the Mill'; in item 'A Papermaker and Machine No.3, page 77. Illustration of recipients at the awards ceremony is on page 162 of this book.

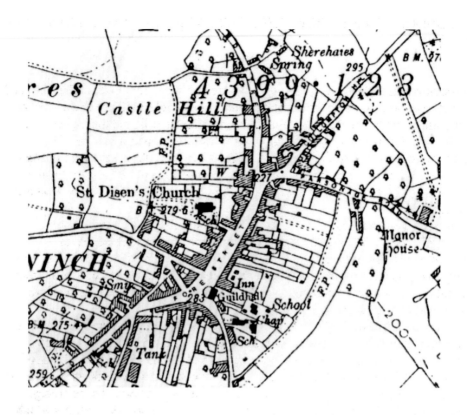

1906 map of the Cullompton Hill area of Bradninch. No.13 is on the right hand side going up out of Bradninch, the one nearest the road of the last pair at the top.

From the 1901 census Violet's grandparents, William and Jane, lived on Cullompton Hill, at no.8; and were born in 1872 and 1874. He worked in the Paper Mill and both had been born in Bradninch. Violet's father, William, was born in 1892.

Going back another generation there were Violet's great grand parents, Robert and Mary at no.5, Cullompton Hill, on the 1901 census and they were born in 1850 and 1851 with Robert born in Exeter and Mary in Bradninch; so that takes the family back to the mid-nineteenth century. He also worked in the Paper Mill at that time of 1901 and associated very much with Cullompton Hill at the turn of the century and before as they were recorded as living there, at no.3, in the 1881 census and he was then a Beaterman in the Paper Mill. As well as two sons there was a daughter, Elizabeth, aged four. She had moved by 1901, then aged 24, to live as a lodger with her brother William and his family at no 8. She was a paper Sorter in the Mill so Violet followed closely in her family occupation.

Violet's knowledge goes back to her grandparent's generation, but the family goes back to the middle of the nineteenth century. With Violet continuing in her family home on Cullompton Hill, this brings the family forward right into the twenty-first century.

28

CHILDHOOD AT PARKVIEW COTTAGES, WORTH – MEMORIES OF JOAN MILLER.

The countryside around Hele, (and here we are talking about those fields, lanes and cottages and farms outside the hamlet of Hele, and especially those to the west at Worth under the lea of Hele Hill, that I knew as Exeter Hill, and the higher Mount of Killerton Park), had a deep quietude with a riotous growth of nature. The hedges were thick and full of flowers, fruit and berries. There were wild flowers everywhere. There were animals and birds in occupation of all the countryside. That is how I recall it in my first ten years of life that I lived at Parkview Cottages at Worth.

My parents were married in 1922. I have two beautiful photographs of the wedding. They were married from a cottage, which was one of a pair, up Hen Street in Bradninch. They have been demolished but were on the right hand side going up (opposite present-day 'Roosters') just before the old pair on the left that are still there. They were set down well off the road and have been replaced by houses and bungalows along the road.

When my parents Edwin (Eddy) and Alice Winter were married they went to live in Worth Cottage, Hele. I understand originally it was two cottages. My sister Margaret was born there. Worth Cottage belonged to Mr. Wellington who also owned Worth Farm. His Aunt came to live with him and went to Worth Cottage so my parents then moved to Parkview Cottages where I was born. Those cottages were on the Worth side of the railway line opposite of Sunnyside Cottages which were over the railway bridge.

Parkview is in Silverton Parish but we went to school in Bradninch. It was over a mile away and as there was no school transport we had to walk the lane that went over Exeter Hill and along West End Road into Bradninch. During the winter months the children who lived in the country areas could leave school earlier so that we could arrive home before darkness fell.

I can remember seeing the wild flowers in the hedgerows and my love of flowers must have stemmed from this. On Sundays after being dressed in our 'Sunday-best' we walked to Church in Bradninch in the morning and after lunch walked to Chapel at Silverton Mill in the afternoon. It was only after that that we could change out of best and into play-clothes and went out to play and let off steam.

The railway line ran along the bottom of the garden and I can remember climbing down the embankment with my parents and sister and walking along the railway line to Silverton Station which was the quickest way. That was on Saturday afternoons, in order to catch the so-called Woolworth Train as it only cost sixpence in old money. In those days it was safe to walk on the railway lines as we knew the times of the trains and there were not as many trains as there are today. We could hear them coming because they were steam engines and the drivers always gave a warning whistle when coming round bends.

My sister made friends with one of the daughters of the Housekeeper in Strathculm House. The Housekeeper was called Mrs.Tanner and she had three children, Ethel, Dorothy and Bob, with Dorothy being my sister's friend. My sister was also friendly with the daughter of the Station Master. She was called Violet Berry and lived in the house on the other side of Hele & Bradninch Station.

I can always remember Harvest time as having picnics in the cornfields. The men working used to pick up the sheaves of corn to make stooks for drying. If I remember correctly there were seven sheaves in a stook. Mr. Wellington used to grow strawberries in his fields and the women used to pick them. I have happy memories of my childhood where it was safe to roam the fields and the sun always seemed to shine.

I remember my first ten years of family life at Parkview. As I mentioned earlier I was the second child of my parents so the time I am remembering was in the late 1920's and early 1930's.

We were in the furthest cottage with my sister and I having a room upstairs. The view was wonderful across the fields and on fine days you could see Dartmoor in the very far distance. We had two framed texts on the wall. They were attractive and the frames were deep, made of wood that were really elaborately carved and I can visualise them still. We sometimes played music up there on an old fashioned gramophone, one that had a large horn to give out the sound. We liked to open the window and place it to the outside. The stairs went up from the front door in the middle of the house, with three bedrooms upstairs but of course no bathroom. Downstairs there was a best sitting-room on one side and the kitchen/living-room on the other, in which was the kitchen range. There were many outhouses, stores and a larder out the back. We of course had our bath in front of the range in a tub brought in from the yard.

There was a long garden in the front and all four cottages were planted in the 'cottage style' with flowers massed together and vegetables. My father was in charge of the pigs for Mr. Wellington and I seem to remember us having one pig kept at our cottage. There were certainly lots of pets that included guinea pigs, rabbits and cats. My father's special interest was his two greyhounds and he was often out exercising them in his spare time. He was very proud of them and of course it was normal in those days to clear the farmland of what was called vermin, be it rats, foxes, badgers, or any other wild animals that interfered with the domestic and farm stock.

The people next to us were called Chappel and the two children were Roy and Betty; in the next cottage Carpenter, and the other end one an ex-Navy man called Salter. There was one pump over a well for all the four homes. In the first cottage of Sunnyside over the railway there was a family by the name of Pepperell. I do remember Mr. Wellington as a tall, large man who often wore a large wide-brimmed hat, a bit scary to me at my young age. The person who had the farm after him was called Mr. Issacs and he had come there from Silverton. The Wellington children were two boys and a girl called Rosamunde. When they did move away they went to Cambridge and some of them were involved with a firm that tested seeds. Miss Wellington, remained at Worth Cottage and she had a housekeeper to look after her called, if I recall correctly, Dorothy Knight; although it was Knight after she married Bill Knight and I did not know her maiden name when she was at Worth cottage.

Some of my memories and information continued from after I was at Parkview

30

because we moved from there to Bradninch when I was ten years of age. We moved into one of the cottages on the right, when going up Cullompton Hill and they have since been demolished. We thought it was wonderful to have a tapped water supply as we had only had a pump at Parkview. I understand the pump is still there.

I still spent my free time out in the countryside and was sometimes back in the Worth Farm area. Also we heard information of people we had known and my husband Graham in his youth had also been involved at Worth Farm. He remembers working out of school time for Mr.Wellington. Boys used to be paid to cut the seed potatoes so that each piece had only two 'growth eyes' so that increased the crop to be planted. Women were also employed on that and the fruit-picking work. The farm had fields of strawberries that were picked by hand. Beyond Worth Farm in the last field before the lane joined Ellerhayes there used to be old railway coaches. They were coloured yellow and brown from their time on the railway and some of the time they were used as storage and to house chickens. At strawberry picking time families came from away and stayed in them while they worked on the farm. My cousin, Lilly Salter, whose maiden name was Winter used to love to come out to visit us while we lived at Parkview and remembers that there were fields of blackcurrants that were picked as well as the strawberries.

We, as children knew all the names of the fields and used them to meet up in. There were so many flowers, and a special one to me was the white violet, prolific on the bank opposite Worth Cottage. There was also the pennywort that when we spat on the leaves to rub them together; and then when thrown into the air opened or remained closed to give us folklore information as to whether it was going to be rain or shine. The leaves remained together for wet atmosphere or opened if it was dry! We had quite a lot of such games with plants. We sometimes roamed down towards Killerton along the river and the woodland area behind the grounds. I remember a large wheel set on the ground that we used to spin round on but I never knew its real purpose.

We always felt free and happy in the countryside except for one place close by. There were a group of large trees at the junction of the Exeter Hill road to Bradninch and Strathculm Road that led down to that big house and the Mill. It was called Potters Elm and we all believed it was haunted. A bungalow has since been built there with the same name.

Thinking back it was probably because the trees created a darker space below the foliage and the noise of the wind in the leaves built up the atmosphere for us children to frighten each other. We had to pass the spot to and from school, there being no other route we could take to avoid it and we would rush by at times.

After leaving Hele I continued at school in Bradninch and afterwards worked for a family at the bottom of Fore Street. I looked after their young child as they owned the Drapers shop and so were very busy. My mother worked in the Paper Mill at Hele and although I was told to have other thoughts on employment as it was hard work, I did go down there later in the paper-testing department. I also remember collecting primroses for the promotion each year when they sent bunches to their customers.

My mother was an excellent needle-woman and made all our clothes. One thing she did was to buy a dress in Exeter that she liked, and at home took it apart and so have a pattern to cut out a second dress to make up, so as to have one each for my sister and me.   Then she would sew the original dress up and we both had new similar dresses. My sister ended up as good a needle-woman and I have always loved producing craft-work. My first love was for Peramano designs on that special paper and they were made into greeting cards. That craft was introduced into this country from the Low Countries in about1921. I then went on to study Honiton Lace and occupied many hours to produce the complex lace patterns. I used my knowledge and love of flowers to design some of the images I made.

Above is the wedding photograph of Joan's parents in 1922. On the following page are two photographs; one of Joan as a small child, the other of her father with his two greyhounds; both taken at Parkview Cottages.

Information notes relating to the area of Worth.

a)   Eddy and Alice were married in 1922 so the family was in one of the cottages at Worth from then, or soon after. He was employed on the Worth Farm being in charge of the pigs. They had to move out to make way for an Aunt of Mr. Wellington. From Jane May's records of the cottages there were two Miss Wellingtons, sisters of Mr. Wellington, at Worth, one in each cottage. After Mr Wellington died it is possible the son took over the farm and an Aunt, sister to his father came to help. Eddy Winter would have continued working for the son.

b)   Worth Cottages were part of Worth Farm in those days. Sunnyside, a row of three cottages, and Park View, a row of four cottages were built on land close by but on the neighbouring farm, Penstone. Most of them now in private ownerships.

c)   Exeter Hill is the local name used in Bradninch and surrounding area for the small hill to the north of the hamlet of Hele. This is because from Bradninch looking westwards the hill is seen in the direct line from the town towards Exeter. In this book and in my previous items I have identified the hill as Hele Hill because it is within the immediate hamlet area and so is part of Hele. Exeter is to the south-west of Hele whereas Exeter Hill alias Hele Hill is to the north of Hele, and obviously Exeter Hill is a name giving a correct sense of direction to the people in Bradninch but not to the residents of Hele.

d)   Potters Elm as a name goes much further back than the name of the bungalow which was built in the second half of the twentieth century. The name was on earlier maps that don't show any dwelling there so it was identifying the road junction with its group of mature trees. When I came into the area I thought that in the past there must have been an old dwelling at that place, with of course a memorable ancient Elm on the site, and along with that, a locally renowned person had lived there who had been a potter; or that pottery making may have been there for some long period of time.   I was told however that obviously a very large Elm had been there but the name Potter referred to a man of that surname who had hung himself from the tree. Not such a pleasant reference and maybe just tale but with a grain of truth in it.

An illustration map of the immediate area and the houses mentioned follows on page 42.

WORTH COTTAGE - INFORMATION FROM JANE MAY.

Worth Cottage was built as two semi-detached cottages. The farmer, Mr. Wellington had two maiden sisters, and in 1918 they moved in, to live separately but side by side. 1918 may have been significant in that it was the end of the First World War and maybe one or both had lost their future husbands in that conflict. They were each always known as Miss Wellington.

At sometime, and I don't know how long after this happened, their brother, of Worth Farm, died while on a fishing expedition at sea off the Cornish coast. This must have been a great loss to them and altered the family situation. A body was washed up onto the beach down in the area of the expedition but before it could be recovered it had gone out to sea again so there was no formal identification and so legally there had to be a wait of seven years before he could be declared dead.

34

The farm was sold but with the two Miss Wellingtons remaining in the cottages. Later the new owner of the farm was given the right to buy the two cottages, presumably when they came empty, and this he did in 1964 for something like seven hundred pounds. He sold them the next day for about three and a half thousand pounds so it seems likely the price he paid for them had been fixed at some earlier stage.

The new owner of Worth Cottages, Mr. Sidney Gregory, was a builder and decorator but his skills were not given to the property. He lived in one small part of it, which was patched up with modern materials that seem to have been left over from other work while the rest was empty and neglected and left to deteriorate. He did some alterations such as removing both staircases and changing doorways to convert into one dwelling. Some of it was used as a storage place and the gardens and outbuildings were full of rubbish with empty tins, building materials and glass everywhere.

He sold it to Michael and myself in 1986 and we found it needed a lot of sorting out as the layout didn't really work as it was. For example the new stairs had to be re-aligned as it was unsafe; and one front door went straight into the garage door if that had been left open. There were rats in the sheds and outbuildings and mice all over the house. Michael and I worked for many years on the house and garden to convert it to an excellent dwelling with a very attractive garden. The garden when we moved in had not been altered from Miss Wellington's time. It ran back behind the house and wide to one side in which there had been a circular pond and tree area. At the top of the garden were many fruit trees and a large soft fruit area that was renowned for its blackcurrants. There were many sheds and a greenhouse so it seemed as though Miss Wellington had been very self-sufficient with a good farming background.

I remembered Worth Cottage from when I was young. It had been empty at times and to the young people around it had gained a reputation of being haunted, although as far as anyone knew no one had ever died there. However living at nearby Ellerhayes with my husband, Michael, who worked at Silverton Mill, we both thought it a very attractive place and decided to buy it when Sid Gregory, in the pub at Silverton, talked of selling up to go back to London. We were able to buy it from Sid and realised our dream.

[Jane is the daughter of Walter Wingrove; whose memories are in a different item in this book.]

RAILWAY CUTTING in the 1840's at WORTH, HELE.

The arrival of the Railway, opened on 1st May 1844 into Devon seems to have created quite an impact on that existing rural community between the Hele and Silverton stations. It was not shown on the Tythe Map of 1841 as it was completed through that part of the Culm Valley after that date. It went through the middle of field no 965, called Pond Close and was laid in a very deep cutting with the lane from Hele to Killerton and the Bridge Mill crossing over it at that point. It seems likely that the two side areas of the field were used by the Railway as site or temporary residence structures for the constructing of the very large cutting and road bridge there.

Those two smallish areas of that field that were left one each side of the railway were never absorbed into adjoining fields but cottages built on them taking up with their gardens exactly the side areas. One side of the railway became Parkview, the other side Sunnyside. At the time the field was under the ownership of Acland who owned the large Killerton Estate of most of the land to the south and west, including the Bridge Papermill. The field was part of either Pitt Farm which was just to the south and the occupier was John Mathews or Penstone Martyn, a farm again just south, occupied by Thomas Martyn. Both men were involved with the ownership and running of the Papermill.

Before that great change there was in the countryside around the area as well as Worth Farm other important dwellings such as Moorland, Clisthayes, Penstone and Yard Farm.

WORTH FARM. The farm had been in existence for many centuries and would need its own separate historical study apart from the interest in the cottages around it generated by the memories of Joan Miller.

In the 1871 CENSUS at the Farm was Thomas and Matha Mary Bessett, and their four children. He had 150 acres employing 4 Farm Servants and 2 Boys.
By the 1881 CENSUS Worth Farm had Frank Challice, on his own with no family. He employed three servants, Sarah Needell, aged 26, Eliza Haydon, aged 15, as Domestic Servants and John Knowles aged 16, as an Indoor Farm Servant.
1891 CENSUS again a change to James and Mary Kembles, and children, Edwin 28; Eli 26; George 23; Anne 20; Jane 19; Harry 14, with the adult sons occupation listed as Farmer's Sons. The 1901 CENSUS shows James and Mary Kemble and all five eldest children had remained at, or returned, home and were by now mature adults but no families of their own

Worth Cottages were built for and belonging to Worth Farm to house its workers and their families.

WORTH COTTAGES as two dwellings. First census in 1881 CENSUS. (cottages built in the previous 10 years.) In one was George and Mary Ann Pearcey. He was an Agricultural Labourer. In the second cottage was George Rew, aged 37, as an Agricultural Labourer, with his wife, Maria, aged 27, and their children, William Henry 5; Elizabeth 3; John 2; George was born in Broadclyst.
1891 CENSUS. In one was James and Sarah Mardon. He was Manager of Coal-yard. In the other cottage was William Rew, aged 48, an Agricultural Labourer, with his wife, Matha, aged 37, and their children, John 16; William 14; Mary 12; Ann 11; Elizabeth 9; Thomas 4; Charles 1; William Rew was born in Broadclist, Matha in Butterleigh, Mary, Ann and Elizabeth listed as Scholars.
1901 CENSUS. William and Matha Rew still in one cottage and he in same occupation. Ann, now 21, the only child at home from 10 years previous. Younger children in the family were, Jane 11; Edgar 8; Leonora 6; Arthur 1.
In the other cottage was John Rew, aged 26, his wife, Elizabeth, aged 25, and son, William, aged 10 months. John Rew was an Agricultural Labourer and the son of William and Matha Rew, as he is shown as aged 16 ten years earlier.

LEASE COTTAGES, which were right down by the river and tucked in close to Bridge Papermill (later called Silverton Mill), were much earlirr cottages because they were on the Tythe Map of 1841. A look at the names and occupations for 1861, reveals there were six dwellings at Lease. Not surprisingly, all the householders worked in the Papermill and were all listed as papermakers. Their names were: John Coleman; George Rookes; Thomas Dart; Thomas Southcott; Francis Issac; Daniel Helson. In the following census of 1871 there were all papermakers in the Lease cottages. These were: Southcott, Issac, Southcott, William, and Slater.

So with the completion of the railway:--

To go from the 1871 CENSUS when PARKVIEW existed (built within the previous ten years) they had three households of Paper Mill workers; John Cooksley, Christopher Haydon and John Bonner and one, Thomas Vinnicombe on the Railway. In 1881 Parkview still had the same occupants except that John Bonner had died and his wife remained with eldest son working in the Paper Mill; but Vinnicombe had moved his occupation from Railway to Agriculture. In 1891 there were two households of Paper Mill workers; William Quick and Sarah Bowden, a Widow, with son, William 16 and she worked at the Mill and two, William Salter, a Platelayer, and John Mitchell, a Signalman on the Railway. In 1901 there was Richard Carpenter in the Paper Mill; and three, William Slater, a platelayer, was still there, Abraham Pepperell, a Porter and Charles Kemp a Signalman on the Railway.

SUNNYSIDE cottages existed by the 1881 census as three dwellings. There were Mill workers in all of them, Arthur Southcott, with two sons as Papermakers, John Oliver and John Southcott. In 1891 all three occupants Daniel Elston, Frank Mortimore and Walter Coles were Mill workers. By 1901 just one change with Francis Lake and William Ireland in the Mill but Albert Harris was a Ganger on the Railway.

This indicates that both Parkway and Sunnyside had no agricultural connection, and most likely had been built for the employees of the Mill, especially as the land on which those two groups of cottages were built had nothing to do with Worth Farm. It could explain their interesting names. Sunnyside Cottages were on the south of the railway; while Parkview was on the north and had an excellent view of Killerton Parkland. It sounds a creative thought-provoking idea and certainly relates more to the Landed or Papermill thinking than to farming names.

An illustration map is on the following page.

In a separate item, 'Cydermaking at Whiteways', page 123, June Bolt is related to the Rew family who were at Worth Cottages, so they are here in greater detail. She refers to them in her memories. A field name at Worth is studied in a separate item, 'Volibeer,' page 46.

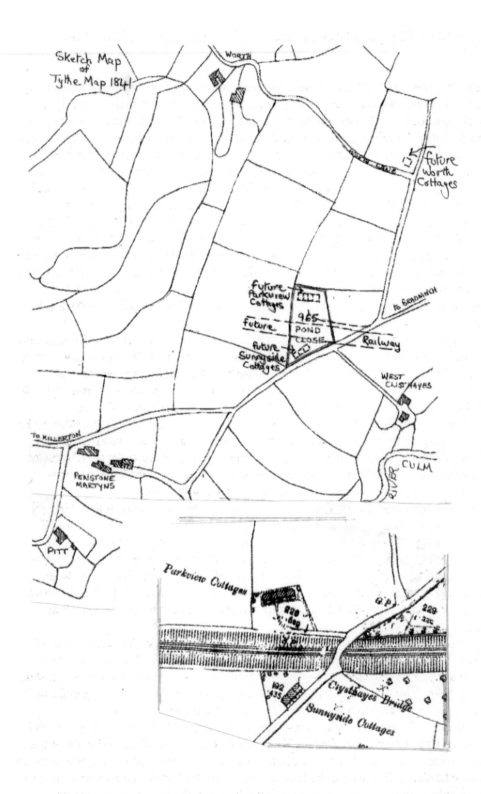

Sketch Map of the 1841 Tythe Map showing field Pond Close no.965. Lower illustration is from an early twentieth century Map, with changes caused by the construction of the Great Western Railway.

38

AROUND THE HILL ABOVE HELE – A PRE-HISTORIC MEANDER.

Hele Hill, the small hill above Hele has been of interest from the beginning of any study of the hamlet. Natural features interacted upon the positioning of early dwellings, roads, and man's industrial activities. The hill today often looks open and bare due to the disappearance of the patchwork of small fields with their heavy dividing hedges of a hundred years ago. In earlier centuries forest may have covered the hill and the lowlands or else maybe the tops of small bare hills rose out from the trees. The map in The Book of Devon Maps of 1809 had a simple clarity that showed the hill rising out of the lowland. Each side of it there was a spring-stream from the higher ridge of hills to the north and those streams ended in the river Culm in its floodplain. On checking the old lanes, tracks and footpaths while at the same time ignoring the dominance of later tarmac routes of today it indicated that pre-Roman routes went around this hill, linking together to completely encircle it. There was also significantly one track from that circle, still visible on the ground, that branched straight off at Worth Cottage of today; going up the hill a short way.

On one of my meanders around the hill I met Mr.Robert Webber, who lives at, and farms, Worth Farm. He was very aware of the history of the farm and surrounding area and knew all the names of the old small fields, including the one named Volibeer, but could not resolve its meaning. (subject of separate item, page 46) He did know of small barrow sites on the land partly due to his farmer's keen knowledge of his soil. Sometimes an expert farmer can notice differences when he works the land; for instance a line or curved shape in a field shows up under the plough or through crops, as more stony or that it drains better or less well than the rest of that area. Mr.Webber did think there was always a possibility of a pre-historic burial barrow under the fields on the hill above Worth.

Looking back at the Tythe Map of 1841, although Worth Cottage was not in existence then, the track starting up the hill at that point was shown. The small field at the end of the track was called Little Down and no more significant than adjoining fields called Western Down and Underhill. However the two very small fields above Little Down were called Higher and Lower Fore Hall. I had taken those names to be an old term to describe their position on the 'Hill' but the word 'Hall' may have represented a link from the past of an earthwork or some land shape.

It inspired me to not only to consider life around Hele Hill in pre-Roman times but to go back to the Register of Devon's Sites and Monuments. I had been there to expand the history of the hamlet of Hele in my first book, Memories from the Mill, (page 159). This time from the map of the Register I looked at where people had settled and how the hill above Hele fitted in or affected issues then.

The pattern of small settlements had been on the slopes of the slight ridge of land between Bradninch and Killerton. That land was just above the flood plain of the Culm river. Those pre-historic settlements could have extended through Bradninch but are harder to find where the land is built upon. Perhaps of equal importance to the people in their choice of site was that they were all close to where spring streams came down from the hills to the north. Bradninch's roots were most likely from pre-historic times and the Saxon settlement was at the present-day junction of Fore Street and Hen Street. That site was on the spring stream running down Hen Street, still there today, although piped under Fore Street and then on to the river Culm.

The records showed there was no settlement on the Hele Hill (at any rate none has been discovered). There was no barrow indicated on the top of the hill either so that suggests the hill was not a burial site although again it may just not have been discovered. So what did the pre-historic people use the hill for! It could have just been a forested hill used for hunting or it may have been a bare hilltop to be used as a meeting place or beacon-point.

I have made notes below of the closest sites, some of which although already noted in my first book are repeated here for ease of seeing the whole picture.

A)   In the field west of Passmore Road, above Cross Cottages. – Various linear marks with a possible rectilinear single ditch enclosure width 20m. Gentle south/east slope, nothing visible.(meaning no raised or surface item) recorded from the air in 1984 Crop mark settlement, prehistoric linear feature recorded 1991; visible 1991.

B) C) Field below Cross Cottages. – Linear features, some meeting at right angles. Settlement, prehistoric. Lies on an even slope. Nothing visible on ground. Recorded from the air in 1984/5, visible 1991. Also Enclosure, prehistoric. Small irregular single ditch enclosure dia. 40m. Lies on gentle south/east slope. Crop mark settlement recorded in 1985, visible 1991.

D)   Field between Hele Payne and Hilly Lane. – Ring ditch, prehistoric. Annular dark mark, dia.10m. no visible mound. Ritual, prehistoric. Linear features nearby probably drainage. Crop mark feature recorded from the air 1989, visible in 1991.

E)   Field east of Worth Cottage, on south/west slope of the hill above Hele. – Ring ditch, prehistoric. Small annular mark dia.10m. site lies on a gentle south slope. Recorded from the air as a crop mark as ritual prehistoric but tall crops concealed any details in 1989. Visible in 1996.

F) Same field as E) but lower flatter area nearer road. – Group of crop marks including circular enclosure of ring ditch dia. 25m.; oval mark dia. 20m. in length and faint part annular mark dia. 20m. Site lies on a gentle south slope. Recorded from the air, tall crop concealed details 1989, visible in 1996

G)   Field behind Sunnyside Cottages over Clysthayes railway bridge. – Ring ditch, prehistoric ritual. Four small circular marks, possibly ring ditches dia. 10m. close together. Other linear features. Field level, no change in soil colour. Seen as crop marks from the air, visible in 1991.

H)   Field along Worth Lane beyond Farm, between lane and Ellerhayes. – Enclosure, rectilinear 15m.x18m. with associated features both linear and circular. Settlement prehistoric. Roman. Site lies on level ground but no visible traces. Recorded as a crop mark from the air in 1990, visible 1995.

I) Field between Worth Farm and Ellerhayes, south of H) north of railway. – Enclosure. Irregular five sided enclosure with linear feature adjacent. Site lies in nearly level field in Culm valley. Visible as a crop mark in 1991.

J) Field on the west side of Ellerhayes. – Ring ditch, prehistoric ritual. Dark annular mark dia. 25m. Site lies on the crest of a north/west ridge. No visible earthworks. Pale zone around the ring ditch is stonier than the surrounding soil and the owner finds it hard to plough and quicker to dry out. Recorded from the air as a crop mark 1995, visible 1996.

K) At junction of Stockwell lane and Silverton Road. – Settlement. A complex area of about 100m by 60m. overall. Probably an enclosure and field system. Lies on a gentle south slope. No visible traces. Seen as a crop mark in 1995, visible in 1996.

L) Close to the hill south of Stockwell Farm. – Enclosure, prehistoric settlement. Small irregular single ditch, with traces of inner circular feature. On an even south/southeast slope. Nothing visible on ground. As a crop mark in 1985, visible in 1991.

M) North of Moorland, and the Bradninch Road. – Enclosures, prehistoric settlement. Parts of two adjacent single ditch enclosures that lie on an east-facing ridge. Also a part curvilinear single ditch which lies on a east/west ridge with a small stream to the north. Nothing visible on the ground. Seen as a crop mark in 1984, visible in 1991.

When those last three sites are added to the ones to the east, south and west of Hele Hill it creates a circle around the hill. Very few sites have been found on the higher ridge of hills to the north (unless they have not all been discovered), that suggests the lower ground closest to the river was the favourable location for occupation. The sites seem to be on land below the 100 foot contour, so maybe these are part of a sweep along the river with Hele Hill just too high for occupation. The primary keys seem to be height of land combined with fresh water and being fairly close to the river. The map following gives a good overview of the area. There were other crop mark sightings on the other side of the river Culm that almost look as though they continued the line southwards. It may be that there was a crossing place over the river somewhere there. Although today we cross the river Culm at the ancient Ellerhayes Bridge, just under the land outcrop of Killerton, there are other old tracks, one towards the river a little way to the east of Penstone Farm; and one opposite on the other side of the river from Beare Farm. It is shown as a route across the river and flood area on the 1809 Map, on page 54, from Martins (old name for Penstone) to Bere (old name for Beare). Dwellings are not prehistoric; they would have come about as the appropriate site for those later centuries, but also as continuing on older settlement sites, long forgotten, as well as the ones recorded in the fields as crop marks.. The completion of a circle of homesteads around the hill is of historical times, but they may overlay the pre-historic pattern of routes around the hill.

On the following page: Map of Hele Hill identifying pre-historic sites from the Register. Followed by two pages of sketch plans in groups East, South, West and North.

Pencil sketch of Hele Hill from the west, across the fields at Ellerhayes is on page IV.   41

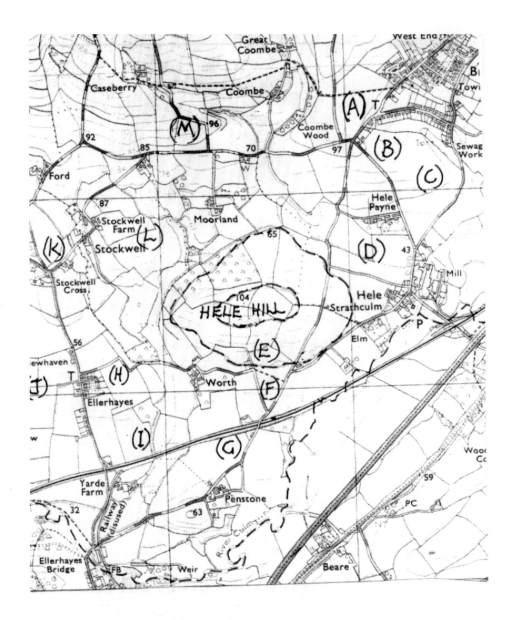

Notes on the Illustration of the 1809 Map on page 45.

The old routes, or tracks, around Hele Hill that could have been used in the distant past show as :-- to the north along road past Great Moorlands; south at Little Moorlands along footpath close to the stream; up the direct Bradninch to Exeter road a little way; down Hilly Lane to Hele centre; up Srathculm Road to Potters Elm; across field by footpath to Worth Cottage; along Worth Lane, past Worth Farm, to right angle in lane before going east to Ellerhayes; follow stream north to Stockwell; along road through Stockwell Farm and continue along road eastwards to the Moorlands road to complete the circle.

The Roman Road went from Bradninch (in the top right corner of the map), along West End Road and cut across Hele Hill to Potters Elm, then Martyns, and on to Exeter (from the bottom left corner of the map).

42

SITES TO THE EAST   SKETCH DIAGRAM OF A) B) C) D)

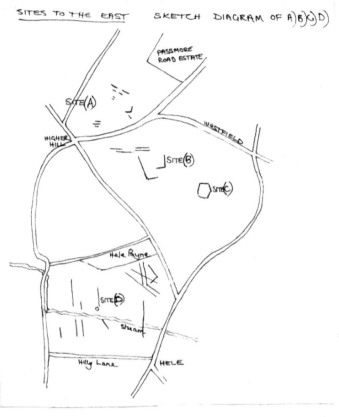

SITES TO THE SOUTH

SKETCH DIAGRAM OF E) F) G)

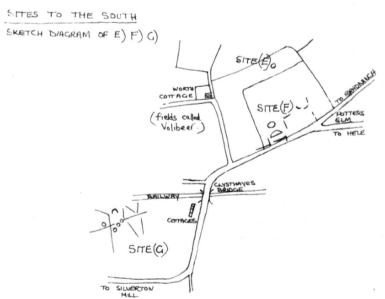

43

SITES TO THE WEST   SKETCH DIAGRAM OF H) I) J)

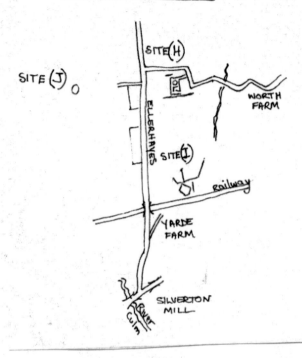

SITE (J) o

SITE (H)

ELLERHAYES

WORTH FARM

SITE (I)

Railway

YARDE FARM

SILVERTON MILL

River Culm

SITES TO THE NORTH   K) L) M)

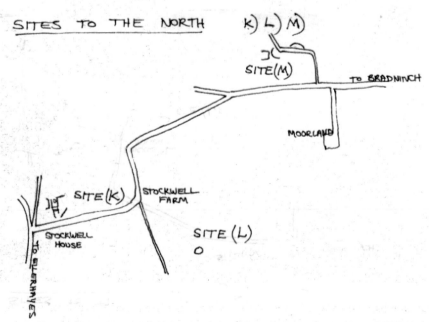

SITE (M)

TO BRADNINCH

MOORLAND

SITE (K)   STOCKWELL FARM

STOCKWELL HOUSE

SITE (L) o

TO ELLERHAYES

Illustration based on Map of 1809. Names on the map are in script so printed here for clarity: from the top; Copy Down, Bradninch, G.t Casebury, Lit.Casebury, High.r Coomb, Low.r Coomb, Stockquil (Stockland), G.t Moorlands, Lit. Moorlands, Hig.r Hele, Hele Mill, East Clist Hayes, West Clist Hayes, Martyns, Pitt, Atherleigh Mill, Bere. Notes on this illustration and possible old routes on page 42.

VOLIBEER. - THE NAME OF A FIELD NEAR HELE HILL.

The area around Hele Hill was divided up into many small fields in past centuries, generally agricultural names such as Pond close, Woodway, Western down, Little down, Barn close, Great mead and Fernclose. One field seemed different to all the more usual ones. It was called Volibeer and was just to the west of Hele Hill.

Old English Place Names give clues to the two parts; Voli to link to wolf, wolf meadow; or wool with sheep and to shear; or a leafy bower or shelter, or directly to the west country, a clump of trees as shelter, to hid and conceal. There is also a possible link to red flowers, violet and the flower viola. From the latin language a possible link to flit about or part of a proper name for a gallic tribe, Volsci ōrum. With regards to the 'beer' part it could have linked to malted barley and a drink; or a buckthorn plant; or to support or carry, to beare the dead to burial.

To follow up the several lines from old meanings there was an instant liking for wolves but not really the most likely; more a leafy shelter or the west country 'clump of trees' or 'a wood grove'; or even Viola flowers. Forgetting sheep sheering and trapping wolves one further book, Flibbert and Skiddicks, Devon Dialect, by Clement Martin the word Vore is used for 'front; along; towards furrow,' from the Celtic word Vor meaning furrow or way through. This seemed a possible meaning as there could have been an old route past Hele Hill. The Register of Devon's Ancient sites listed a possible Roman Villa site on the same lane past Volibeer field beyond Worth Farm. Taking it that it is known that a Roman route to Exeter went approximately along the road south of Volibeer, then the lane alongside Volibeer could have been part of a linking track, or so called Vor or way through to the villa. Maybe the Romans also trapped wolves there or sheared sheep!

Remembering that the Mount of Killerton is the remains of the cap top of the core of an ancient extinct Volcano there is however a more romantic possibility. In the distant past the land around Killerton must have been very fertile after eruptions and lava flows. To link to the mid-twentieth century, there were flowers grown commercially at Worth for the perfume industry. The situation is excellent in that it is facing south and protected under Hele Hill. There was water in the area as a stream runs around the hill passing through Worth to the river Culm, one of several from springs in the line of hills to the north, renowned for their fine quality; one in Silverton called 'heal eye stream'.

On the Tythe map of 1841 at Worth one field (no.2001) called Poppy Mead; another called Cherry Park (no.976); one called Nursery (no.996), and many small orchards. The name Worth itself which may have indicated high quality soil. So maybe Volibeer is a plant name, so back to more normal agricultural terms after all; its root from the Welsh, Fiola and Fioled meaning the plant Viola. It springs to mind the longstanding famous Devon Violet perfume sold all over the world. In the more distant past plants were seen as herbs and medicine, the scent of flowers having beneficial health value as well as religious and spiritual value. Maybe the 'beer' part of Volibeer meant that Old English beer or some brew was made from the plants grown at Worth. Two adjacent field names called Great Bitter Mead and Little Bitter Mead (nos. 998, 999) give us an inkling of herbs, and fortifying drinks. Hops were added as a preservative to the basic barley of beer but also its bitter taste; alternatively those two field names might have described an aspect such as a very acid soil. In all I find the plant definition a nice thought, but there remains the possibility of a way through and also an ancient burial ground.

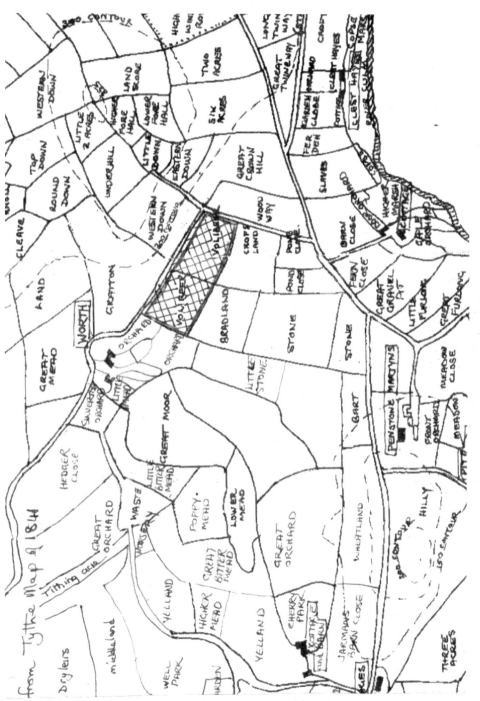

Diagram map from the Tythe Map of 1841 of Silverton Parish of the area of Worth, with field names added. Volibeer field marked hatched for clarity.

MEN IN THE MILL – EARLY PHOTOGRAPHS FROM 1904.

In my first book 'Memories from the Mill' (page 25) there are illustrations of two photographs of the Salle in 1904. They show the women finishing and packing the paper. They wore long skirts with long white aprons. Four more of those rare small snapshots have come to light, reproduced here as original size.

 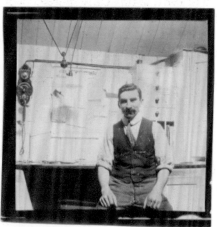

Top left – J.P.Hepburn. Oct. 1904. Hepburn was the Manager and a member of the family that owned the Mill. He is seated in front of his desk in his Office, with a notice-board and drawers behind him. There can be seen the message pulley system that they must have used, it looks similar to those that used to be in Department Stores in the early twentieth century. He is dressed formally in suit, tie and stiff white collar.

Top right – Petrie. Oct. 1904. Petrie photographed in the same position. It is assumed he was in charge of an important work area in the Mill. He is quite formally dressed but in shirt, tie, stiff white collar and waistcoat. He has his sleeves rolled up workmanlike.

Bottom left – Joey at Hele. 1904. That one is faded but shows one worker, presumably 'Joey', next to the end of a papermaking machine.

Bottom right – Petrie, Glass. J. Squire. June 1904. Photograph was also taken next to the papermaking machine. Petrie, on the left, dressed as in his individual photograph. The other three workers, in collarless shirts, sleeves rolled up and braces to their trousers.

WORKING LIFE AT HELE – MEMORIES OF WALTER WINGROVE.

I started work at the age of fourteen, the Monday following the end of the school term after I had reached that age. It was at Easter-time. That was in 1932 and I retired in 1981, taking early retirement at the age of sixty-three. So there was for me forty-nine working years in my life.

My father was also called Walter but whereas his second Christian name was John, mine is Albert. He had worked at the Hele Paper Mill, and so when I left school I started on my working life there as Lodge-Boy. We lived in Fore Street, three doors down from The Castle Hotel that is still there next to the Guildhall. I cycled to work.

The day started at 7.00 a.m. and I had to be there to pull the rope to ring the bell that was set high on the roof of the Mill. That was the 'start bell'. I had to ring it also for the start and end of the lunch break and end of day at 5.00 p.m. If I didn't make it in time in the morning then Frank Miller, the Lodge-Keeper did it and he then told me off. On Saturdays the hours were from 7.00 to 11.45 a.m. so I worked a 48 ¾ hour week and as the pay was 2⅞ pence an hour ended with 10 shillings a week. We are talking old money here with wage increases worked out in half farthings although there was no such coin.

My next job of the day was to sweep out the Lodge and then light the fire. The Lodge was a small stone building at the old gate entrances. It was divided into two with two doors from the road; we were in one side with a corner window, to watch the entrance gates, a counter and a fireplace. The other side was like a passage with a large clock with a fixture under it that held a large roll of paper that the workers stamped their number and the time onto and then went on in or out. One of my jobs was to call out that information from it and Frank would record it all in a ledger so that the hours and any overtime could be checked before pay-day each week.

To go back to the start of the day however – I had to chop kindling wood to light the fire. If I used too much on the fire Frank would take some off; he was tight on that. We had a side-line in that for firewood I had to chop up the old wooden barrels that had held liquid resin. The resin was used in the Mill to stop the belts that were on the machines from slipping. Any spare wood was sold to the work-people for 3 pence a bag, and they used to put an extra 3 pence on the bench for me as I had done the hard work.

The next job was important in that I had to go up to the Post Office in Bradninch to collect the mail. I went on my bike, and now I come to think of it, I provided the vehicle and there was no thought of any maintenance cost being paid to me. Perhaps I should have taken more time over the job and walked the mile there and back again. I had to repeat the job in the afternoon to take mail going out from the Mill to the Post Office. The Post Office in Bradninch was towards the lower end of the High Street. It included with it the next premises down which was the Bakery side of the business. On the other side of High Street there was the Newsagents, owned by Mr. Harris, who was an expert photographer, he did all the weddings and special events. The shop had continued as a newsagent until a few years ago when it closed and was converted into a house.

When I was in my first position as Lodge-Boy they were still using horses to pull the wagons of coal from the railway into the Mill, and for moving everything about the Mill in carts. In fact it was a very noisy environment with the noise of the cart-wheels rumbling about. The saying in Bradninch by the old folk of the time was that they knew when the wet weather was coming as the atmosphere changed when they heard the trains on the railway and the trucks being pulled into the Mill at Hele.

There were three Shire horses at work so back at the mill I had another task that occurred throughout the day. It was my responsibility to sweep the yard within the Mill entrance every day and of course if the horses left a pile in that area I had to go out at once and collect it up into a bucket. If I didn't notice then Frank would very soon tell me. Frank did the gardening in the Mill and I had to put the horse manure onto the rose beds he looked after in front of the main offices in the yard. The three horses were looked after by Tom Bond, Bert Power and Richards (I have forgotten his first name); each man took care of and worked an individual horse. Tom got badly hurt at one time when one of the horses kicked him and he was off work injured for a long time but I think he did come back. The only really bad casualty that was remembered from my father's time was Bill Laity who was killed in the Mill on the railway sidings that came into the Mill from the main line railway. The horses were pulling the trucks full of coal and they moved backwards suddenly for some reason and he was trapped between the trucks.

There were rows of racks for bikes in the yard just behind the Lodge as a lot of the workers used bikes; otherwise it was using your feet to get to work. In winter we seemed to get times of harsh weather. We still had to get to work and Bradninch is so hilly it was very slippery going down High Street and round the corner into Hele Road. There was never anything put on the road to help you get a grip and the children sliding down for fun made it a lot worse. Buses used to have to forget about Bradninch altogether. They would not turn off to Hele but go straight along the main road, past the Merry Harriers, which we always called The Merry Dogs, to Cullompton. Sometimes the snow was to hedge-height near the Red House at Hele. I used to wear socks over the top of my boots to give me a bit more grip on the frosty icy mornings. There has been recorded in the Mill of a fall of large snowflakes in June and it settled in the entrance of the workshops.

There were a lot of different jobs alongside the main papermaking skills. The Hele Square was there with the houses for work people; the Mill also owned houses in Bradninch in Westfield and several other areas; so the Mill employed carpenters, plumbers and maintenance staff. Jock Collier cleaned out the boilers. It would be good to list all the names of the individual jobs that were there when I started.

We used to have to take our own food for breakfast and the mid-day lunch. In a room below the Beater-Room there was an oven in which we could heat our food. There were urns of hot water heated from a boiler also down there, which we could use for making tea throughout the shifts. There was a canteen later on after the war that was good with meals for all the shift workers if they wanted it.

In my father's time they had two 12 hour shifts, from 6 a.m. to 6 p.m. and 6 p.m. to

50

6 a.m. On the weekend it was shut down and a good turn round was from 6 a.m. on Saturday to 6 p.m. on Sunday if changing from nights to days. Some of the men used to go straight from work at 6 a.m. to the White Lion pub in Bradninch for cider or beer before going home to sleep. Maybe they said they missed their evening drink as they were back on shift at 6 p.m. or else the work had made them extra thirsty. The drinks were often marked up on the slate in the White Lion and on payday they would go and pay it off; but on that day they went reeling home and 'the slate' would have started again.

My father had a great knowledge of the working ways in the Mill in his time. He told me of the mills he had worked in before coming to Devon. While he was at Gravesend he said that like a lot of paper-mills the water they used in the process used to come in from the river. One time the whole system came to a halt as nothing was coming in the inlet pipe and it was discovered that an eel was stuck in it thus blocking the supply. Sometimes he would see very small fish in the supply tank but that was because the grill in the river must have disintegrated. Hele Mill also used the river water but for its best quality paper it also used the better spring water from Hele Payne Farm, which was piped to a separate supply tank.

I can remember as a very young boy running to meet my father on payday as he always gave me a penny. He had to retire early through ill-health, I think in 1925 when he would have been about forty-seven, and I was only seven. Before that we had good family times with him playing the violin, my mother and sister both playing the piano and us all singing together.

I had some good times linked to work. There were several sports you could do such as football and cricket and tug of war. The men would travel quite a distance to play or watch, even going to Sidmouth in a cart; rather a bumpy ride. In my father's younger time he told me there was even more football and cricket played than in my time. In Bradninch we kids used to play football one street against another street in makeshift matches.

A favourite activity I joined was the Gym-club, which was held once a week after work in the building in the Square that had been the Chapel in earlier times. To me at my young age there was a lot of equipment such as a horse, rings, and weights. I really went for it and after my first session I was so stiff the next day I could hardly do my work. I learnt to box there and did get fully knocked out once; the going out was O.K. as I didn't know it was happening but the coming round was unpleasant as the surroundings were all swirling around me. Stanley Heal ran the club and he was an excellent athlete. He was nick-named 'Magic' as he could do the gymnastics so well; in fact if he was bored at work looking after his paper machine he walked along the full length of the machine floor on his hands to pass the time and keep in trim.

The workers at the Mill liked to use the pub opposite the Hele railway station; it was then called The Railway Hotel. The landlord at one time was called Sprague. It was very popular in the evenings, a lively bar room, with regulars walking or going on their bikes from Beare, Ellerhayes, and all the farms around as well as people from Hele. At the weekends some brought instruments and it was like a 'sing-a-long' of today with each person always singing their same song. There was one popular one I remember word for word starting with – 'Knock, knock, knock at Flannigan's door' sung by Jack Fowler, and we all knocked on the table in time with the singing. Another one was about George White with – 'every night used to go out courting, George stuttered so much it's true, it took him half an hour, to say I love you'. Although I had been a choir-boy I didn't feel confident enough to sing any special song myself, but I did join in with everyone else. I also played bagatelle.

For us who had came off shift at 10.00 p.m. during the week and men who visited it from Bradninch of an evening we could ride our bikes from the Railway Hotel in Hele when it closed at 10.30 p.m. and get up to the White Lion for another drink before that one closed at 11.00 p.m. The difference in their closing-times was to do with them being in different licensing areas with different arrangements. The Railway Hotel had always been an important, busy place especially when the monthly, or it may have been weekly at some time, market was held. This was on the ground opposite the pub with pens for the animals and all the local farmers used it.

Being Lodge Boy could only last until you were sixteen. I went on to work in the Salle, and then the Stock-room. The paper used to go out from the Mill by railway. The trucks were pulled right through the Mill to the Stockroom. They would be weighed in the Railway yard on the way out and likewise the coal-trucks coming in full of coal would also be weighed. This checked there was no fiddling of fuel or paper. I moved from that to going on the Cutters for the finishing processes before advancing onto the Paper Machine itself. At first I had to collect all the scrap paper and put it to be used again and gradually was taught the various skills leading up to being in charge.

I went on to end up as Supervisor of No. 3 Machine. British and American Tobacco Company owned it by then and I think they were better to the workers with regard to the pay and conditions than the earlier Wiggins Teape firm. In fact I got given not only my presentation of a gold watch for thirty-five years service but at the same time B.A.T. gave me the presentation gift for my fifteen years of service that Wiggins Teape hadn't got around to do.

I didn't mind being a Supervisor even though you were on call. I lived in Townlands, in Bradninch, and when there was a breakdown of my machine and I was at home a man would come up for me; even in the night he had to come and wake me to go and see to it. This used to wake the neighbours so in the end the Mill installed a phone in my house. If I was up in the night then I used to go in late the next day. Otherwise we were there by 8.30 a.m. every day for a meeting to hear how the machines had gone on from the day before and what was to be done that day.

I remember several Managers during my time. There was Mr. Richardson, Mr. Savage, Mr. Worridge in 1960 and Mr. Trail. The Mill produced paper for several important firms and government offices. We made the paper that was the base for Bakelite and Formica. We also produced the overlay paper that was the top layer for Formica and that had to be of very fine quality and sealed before it was made into kitchen unit surfaces. There were experiments with making paper for mats in hotel bathrooms, crepe for food storage and special paper for filters and batteries. These inventive uses of paper took a long time to perfect. Later the base paper technology was sold to Japan and the overlay to Canada. They had a few problems in Canada and I was asked to go there and sort it out but I didn't want to go. I didn't like travelling away but did go to a few of our customers in this country. I was interested in what the paper from Hele ended up as. There was the printing of stamps on our paper for the Post Office at Harrisons at Glory, near Birmingham and the security was very tight there as even paper that was half printed or slightly misprinted would have been useful to counterfeiters. Sandersons, the famous wallpaper manufacturers, was another customer and I visited their works in Wembley. I was told of some orders they carried out for people that wanted totally individual paper and were willing to pay £300 per roll and the design destroyed afterwards so that it was never printed for anyone else. I did go to the Dover paper mill for Wiggins Teape for six months. This was to learn about the plastic base paper for Formica as it was made at the Dover mill before we began it at Hele.

The second world war interrupted my forty nine years of work for six years when I was twenty-one. That world event did produce one domestic alteration to my life in that I met my future wife and we married and I became a family man. Dorothy, who came from Leeds, a real city girl, was working as a Land Girl near Colchester while I was there in the Army and maybe otherwise our paths would never have crossed. Dorothy came to Devon after we were married.

In 1939 Wiggins Teape sent down someone from Head Office to hold a meeting in the old Chapel in Hele Square to try and recruit and start up a Territorial Army group in the Mill and it may have sounded exciting but I didn't join. There were other units in the area locally. Those that did join were the first to be called up at the outbreak of war. There was one unusual event that I've always remembered from just before the war. We didn't hear many planes in those days so when one came over quite low we all left the Packing-room where we were working at the time and rushed outside to look. The next day we were called into the Salle Foreman's office and informed he had evidence that we had been away from our work. The evidence was that it had been the Under Manager who had been up in the plane; he was being taught to fly by the Ministry, and he had taken a photograph of us as his proof! Ironically when the time came to call him up he was found to be unfit for war duty.

They would not let Mr. Richardson, the Manager join up. Paper was needed to be made during the war and although he couldn't make a roll of paper like we machine-men could I suppose he had the skills to organise the production. Before the war there was a great deal of separation between the Management and the workers. We had to show a lot of respect to them, with The Manager always called Sir; but not only that, we also had to be careful not to upset the older workers. Also to get a job in the mill at Hele you were taken on if you were known to the men already there, and they thought you were respectful and not going to cause trouble. In those times in the thirties keeping a job was so important that it kept you in line as families were dependent on all their members contributing. My father was dependent on a small disability pension so it was the family situation as well as your own that you could disrupt by not keeping to your place. It was very different after the war and we could be far more outspoken.

During the War I was in the Army at first as a Signals Instructor and then was transferred to the Navy when we were needed there. I travelled a lot and often in the Mediterranean, doing a lot of escort work. One lucky break came when we were there and had unloaded the ship of its ammunition for it to have a refit, and we were to be sent to Cyprus for a rest time, when we had to quickly re-load and escort a ship from Gibraltar back to Liverpool. We docked on the twentieth of December and I got leave and so spent one unexpected Christmas at Home.

When I retired from the Mill it was at a time when jobs were being cut and it was either me or my direct boss to go. We both wanted to go as the retirement package was better than going on a couple of more years to sixty-five and I was given the choice and so it was that Roy Norman stayed on. I left after the national budget of that year and very luckily tax changes in that meant that instead of tax being deducted from the redundancy I got the full amount. I guess there may have always been problems about the work force numbers that were needed at any time, maybe often due to market forces. In my early years it was known that men were set off at the age of twenty-one when they moved from youth to mens wages. Today my son has taken early retirement with the present owners, Mead, laying off a lot of men in redundancy packages for a second time within a year. He has completed thirty-five years at Hele and the new contract for the workers staying on was a forward contract of two years with no account in any future lay-off redundancy of the earlier employment years.

I did not know of all my family history when I was a lad at school; I was too busy learning how to live; but research has unearthed that the Wingrove family has had continuous links as papermaking workers from as far back as 1740. That is really something to think about as papermaking started in this country around that time. The earlier generations were not in Devon and also moved about the country and even up to Scotland to various paper-making areas. I heard that my father came to Devon as a child with his mother and father and brothers and sisters. My grandmother was at Lease Cottages which were very near Bridge Mill along the river from Hele. Perhaps my grandfather worked there on arrival in Devon. My father worked at Hele Mill after the rest of the family moved away. My uncle Bertrum who had gone back to Kent to a paper-mill at Torvil used to come down to visit. He seemed very rich to us as he had the large white five pound notes on him to spend and what emphasised it to me was that he wore spats above his shoes. The last papermaker in my family with the name of Wingrove was my son, John, who ended his work at Hele with his early retirement in February 2002. I have still got a grandson, Reith, working in a local paper mill – Reed and Smith in Cullompton but he is my daughter's son and has the surname May. My daughter's husband, Michael, worked for many years at Silverton Mill right up until it closed in the year 2000. There may be other branches of the family about in other parts of the country but they have not followed the same papermaking skills continuously that I, and my direct ancestors, did. Locally the mills have closed one by one from

Trews Mill in Exeter, to Stoke Canon, and now Silverton along the river all gone. There is only Hele and Cullompton Mills left.

There were other links into families that were involved at Hele. My sister, Lillian, married Bill Andress who was trained as an electrician under Mr. Thomson, then followed him as the Mill's electrician. The Andress family lived in the Square at Hele and his father, also known as Bill, was Postmaster there and his sister Katie followed her father in that position. She was a very well-known personality in that small enclave of houses until she retired in old age.

Up in the big house, Strathculm, there was a family called Thorold. I've looked them up in the 1934 directory and he was called John Leofrie Thorold, a retired clergyman. The house was not connected to the running of the Mill by then. They had three gardeners with a Mr. Pring as head gardener; and the gardens extended all along the north side of Strathculm Road and that supplied them with fruit and vegetables all the year. There were a few servants in the house as well. There was a tennis court on that side of the river and we used to love playing. I often played with Jack the assistant engineer. I have been on several family holidays to New Zealand as my niece lives over there. While there I felt a link to my past as I watched the restoration of some steam engines; maybe it fascinated me because I had been around machinery all my working life.

Illustration of the Yard, Office House and Mill Buildings at Hele Mill in the 1950's.

There was in direct line from father to son as papermakers recorded from John Wingrove (born 1769) to the present year with John Wingrove (retired 2002). The direct line does go back to Stephen Wingrove (born 1650) as most likely being a papermaker but with no precise written evidence available.

To begin with Stephen; all we know is that he and the next three generations were born in Beaconsfield in South Buckingham. The name Wingrove has several interpretations but the most obvious one is as an old English name from simple nature terms with 'win' for meadow and 'grove' for a stand of trees and describes where a tribe or group of people lived in the past. It is a very common name from Buckingham in the High Wycombe area. Within that area today there is village called Wing and a close-by hamlet called Grove so it would be appropriate to link to there. Records disappear from the distant past so it can be linked in our minds only.

The three generations following Stephen were his son Edward (born 1674), Edward's eldest son Richard (born 1703), and Richard's son Richard (born 1737). That area in which they lived was a very early place for the conversion of grist mills to paper-making with thirty-three such works on four miles of the river Wye there. We could assume the family moved from agricultural work into the Mills as the second Richard had moved to Wooburn before his son, John, was born (born 1769). Wooburn was close to Beaconsfield and is known to have had an early paper mill and John, the next generation, was listed there in a document as a papermaker. Remaining at Wooburn the third son of John, named Richard (born 1793), was a papermaker.

With that last Richard we find the family starting to move away, for a time, from their roots. His eldest son Samuel (born 1816) was born at Horton. This was still close into the same area and had a paper mill. Sarah the first wife had died about 1825 soon after the birth of their fifth child; Samuel being nine at the time. Richard, with or without his young children, moved a long way (especially in those days) to Newcastle and re-married in 1829. His second wife was called Margaret and he had a second family of three children. There seemed to be success there with all the children in the family including the two eldest sons from the first marriage, as separate families in the same locality of Scotswood in 1841 and all the male adults in the family listed as papermakers. This was near Newcastle and was renowned for papermaking and it is recorded that a partnership was formed between Richard Wingrove and a Lawrence Hewison to produce white paper that was in great demand but was little produced. Most paper prior to this was off-white but industrialised businesses were wanting a certain amount of quality paper. That local area of Scotswood was called Wingrove, with a large house of the same name, although there was never any family of the name recorded as resident in it. Also a hospital built there was named Wingrove Hospital.

To remain at that northern location does not follow the line to Devon and Hele Mill but a different interest does crop up that cannot be passed by and may explain the dismissal of the house. The members of the second family turned to the Mormon religion. Richard with their eldest daughter Mary Ann emigrated to America in

1851 with his wife Margaret and the youngest child followed in 1854. Richard the middle child remained in England. Mary Ann married and the family 'crossed the plains' to the Mormon land at Utah. A whole book could be written about that family line but it is enough to say here that they trekked in a wagon-train drawn by oxen. The going was tough with them walking beside loaded wagons. Mary Ann lost a baby daughter and a young son who were buried along the way. Also most tragically Mary Ann was killed when her clothes got caught on the wagon wheels and she was crushed under it so she didn't make it across but her one remaining son did and a large family descends from her there.

However the family line we are tracing is through Samuel who was the eldest son of Richard's first family. In fact the time in Newcastle doesn't amount to more than the early adult years in Samuel's life. By the time of the birth of his seventh child, Thomas, (born 1851) Samuel being then thirtyfive had moved to Dartford in Kent. There were five more children in the family all born there. Dartford was famous for its paper mills and the fine paper they produced. Papermaking had really taken off and Dartford Mills were well into developing machinery for the continuous process of production alongside the older hand made method of earlier times. Samuel became a specialised paper-finisher and his brother, William, who had joined him was a papermaker.

Thomas, the first child to be born at Dartford, became a papermaker at nearby Lower Torvil Mill. He married Mary Ann Hadler and they had six children there before they moved to High Wycombe in about 1892. This, although they may not have realised it, was a return to their family roots. Before 1899 the family had another long distance change to a completely new part of the country. They moved to Bradninch in Devon. It is recorded that he worked at Etherleigh Mill. (later known as Silverton Mill). Three more children completed the family with the youngest born in Bradninch.

Unfortunately Thomas died in 1899 aged 48 and that must have made things difficult for the family in that new venture. By 1910 the family had had more sorrows and separated out. One son had died aged nineteen, also one daughter aged seven, after an accident in Exeter; one adult son returned to Torvil; while the mother with the remaining children except the third adult son, Walter John, (born1878) went north to Rishton in Lancashire. Walter John stayed in Bradninch and he, like his predecessors, became a papermaker and he worked at Hele Mills. Walter married Fanny Daniells, from a Bradninch family, and they had four children with the only son being Walter Albert. It is he who has given us the details of his working life at Hele Paper Mill. The Wingrove line of papermakers goes on down to his son, John, who has also worked all of his working life up until this year of 2002 at papermaking at Hele.

The illustrations on the following page are of Walter's family, most likely his father at work in a paper mill (not known if at Hele.)

THE RIVER CULM BETWEEN HELE MILLS AND KENSHAM MILLS.

An excellent, detailed map of the river and land between Hele and Kensham, in Bradninch, has a great deal of information on it, and is also an item of beauty in itself. Undated, it has to be presumed to be of the mid-nineteenth century.
Title Heading:
'BRADNINCH DEVON. A plan of lands and streams between Kensham Mills and Hele Mills also showing proposed alterations of footpath leading from Hele to Kensham Mills.
Note. Property belonging to the Duchy of Cornwall Colored Green. Property belonging to William Joynson Esqr. Colored Pink.' [old spelling of coloured]
It identified a realignment of a footpath between the two Mills, with the boundaries of the landowners as The Duchy of Cornwall who owned the Mills and land at Kensham, Bradninch; and William Joynson was owner of the Hele Mills and land adjoining it. From documents that gave the history of Hele Mill it is known that Joynson bought it in 1852/3 for his son-in law Charles Collins, so that would be the earliest date for the map. Charles Collins retired from the mill in 1883, so the map and the footpath change was between 1852 to 1883. On the map R.C.Campion Esq. was the owner of the land to the south of the river.
The title heading indicated that both Mills were known in the plural. On the Tythe Map Apportionment list of 1841 the mills at Kensham were called Lower Heynsham and Heynsham Mill, names most likely used from older documents.
From the map: firstly, the shape and line of the River Culm.
The river flowed downstream from Kensham to Hele. Comparison of this map with an ordinance map of 1906 the river Culm in that area remained the same convoluted line at the easterly end towards Kensham. However at the westerly end prior to it entering Hele Mills on this map there was a very large S bow that folded back on its self covering a lot of land. By 1906 this had altered and the river had straightened itself through this S with field shapes changed, with an extra small field on the north side. It would be interesting to know if the landowners patiently waited for nature to change the landscape or whether a helping hand from workmen re-aligned the river.

Secondly, the names of the fields.
The fields were numbered, and responded to the Tythe Map of 1841. The names were given in beautiful handwriting, done by someone used to map-making. For this alone it is worth here a copy from the actual map instead of a diagram. To aid identification field names from Hele to Kensham are as follows:
To the north of the river: Back Orchard, Back Door Close, Capes First Field, Capes Meadow, Goosehill Meadow, Goosehill, Middle Meadow, Long Mead, Burrough Marsh.
To the south of the river: Weir Marsh, Lower Marsh, Higher Marsh, Eight Acres Marsh, Five Acres Marsh.
The ones identified as marshland were next to the river mainly on the south bank as the river flooded mainly that way. It spread over the north bank as the flood levels

rose.   The marsh fields were crossed by many small streams and ditches plus the small tributary river, the Weaver, to drain water into the river when the river was not doing the reverse and spreading out across the land. The fields were, and still are, rich feed for cattle as long as animals were moved to safety in the flood times. Meadow fields were to the north and again were kept as grassland for cattle. Other names raise interest; Back Orchard and Back Door Close were obvious in that they were directly behind what was an old longhouse farmstead called Venmans which had been on the edge of Hele Mills, and had been there prior to the Mill turning from grist-milling to papermaking. Capes First Field and Capes Meadow could have been named after an owner of those and other fields further north, although Capes is an unknown surname to me. Maybe there was a plant called Cape.

Then there was Goosehill and Goosehill Meadow; the first definitely on rising ground from the river plain; maybe in the centuries before a dwelling had been there that maintained a living on geese. Today the small field that has been created by the straightened line of the earlier S bow in the river, just east of Hele Mill, is known today as Hele Marsh and is a very natural wetland. A stream from the spring on the other side of Hele Road arrives there into the river. The field next to it, Goosehill Meadow, is often waterlogged in winter. Flocks of migratory water birds rest there, predominant in them is the GreyLag Goose. Large flocks in V-formation fly over Hele, making raucous noises, and veer to the area in question. It may have been a known place in earlier centuries where geese fed and rested in the winter and as people had to live more directly from natural resources the field names identified that wildfowl position.

On Simpson's survey for the Duchy Of Cornwall of 1788 the field named Goosehill was identified the same as on this map. That survey showed a small building, maybe a dwelling or else an agricultural building on that field but there is no evidence of it on later maps. The field north of Goosehill (not identified on this footpath map) was named Gunpark, again maybe identified to the wildfowl of the mashes as today's Park Farm, at Kensham, is on the old Park (old term for hunting ground) of the Manor of the Royal Duchy in the area. To move further along there was Long Mead, which was divided into strips as hay meadows, let out for the summer months with no disturbance of the soil allowed for crops. Those divisions marked on this map, and also on the Tythe Map; each one lettered and numbered, G 24 to D 17. After Long Mead was Borrough Marsh, right between two branches of the river at Kensham; maybe it was linked to the Town of Bradninch or had been named after an earlier owner.

Thirdly, the road between Hele and Bradninch.

The purpose of the map was to re-align a footpath between the two Mills. To consider the footpath first – the Mill owners and maybe Hele Payne Farm needed to communicate between each other. Going back in centuries this would often have been by physical means; that is someone going to the other place with items or messages. Maybe the Lodge-boy sent on an errand. Now a direct route saved time and also prevented the boy from going through the town of Bradninch which as well as being a longer route had diverse interests to delay him.

The route of the original footpath ran so close to the river edge through Capes Meadow and Middle Meadow that in winter floods it would not have been possible to keep to it. The proposed new route of the footpath was further from the river and on higher ground. It must have, however, interfered with the hay plots of Long Mead as it cut right across them all instead of going along their southern boundary. Maybe the people who rented those strips didn't have any clout to oppose the plan. To return to the Hele end of the footpath. On old maps Hele Payne did not link by road down to Hele Road as at the present day Red House junction; that route was only a footpath. From the farm there were three access tracks; one went west to Back Road and to Exeter with a branch off down Hilly Lane to the centre of Hele; another went north up Higher Hill towards Silverton; and one went straight eastwards to Bradninch across the field and met the Hele Road on the straight length west of the dip and sharp bend, which had the common name of Devil's Corner, where it crossed the spring stream. The start of that last track to Hele Payne was shown on the map as two dotted lines near there.

On the later 1906 map a footpath was shown from Hele Payne to Hele Road along roughly the same line, so maybe an old well-worn route remained when the access track was removed and later still the fields were made into one large one as it is today. Across that beautiful field as it sweeps down to the Hele Road there is a flattened area across it on that old track line and it can be imagined that old hedgerows went along each side of the track to the farm. All those old footways have not been in use for a very long time; but at least a puzzle of the landscape can now be understood.

To follow the old and new footpaths on that Mill map, the old one started on Hele Road west of that Hele Payne track at the boundary hedge between Back Door Close and Capes First Field, marked with an X. The start of the new footpath on the map was to be further along Hele Road towards Bradninch, east of the Hele Payne track, towards the end of Capes First Field, marked with a Y. Up to about twenty years ago, there used to be a gateway into that field at about that place and that still shows as a weaker patch in the thickness of the hedge with newer additional fencing. Following along the lines of the old and new footpaths on the map, the old went straight down to the river, along it across Capes Meadow, across Goosehill Meadow, right on the river bank again at Middle Meadow and lastly on the lower river edge of Long Mead to exit on the Park Farm track, marked Z, which linked to Kensham Mills. The new footpath cut diagonally across Capes First Field, tight under the top hedge of Goosehill Meadow and Middle Meadow, and diagonally across the centre of the Long Mead hay strips to end at the same exit as the old route. The 1906 map, showed part of Long Mead as a Cricket Ground and Pavilion, so it was possible that Long Mead as well as Burrough Marsh were linked to the townspeople of Bradninch. Kensham Mills finally closed down after a disastrous fire in 1892 so Hele Mills didn't send the Lodge-boy with messages any more. The countryside and footpaths between the two Mills was most likely ignored.

Illustrations of the nineteenth century map of the River Culm and proposed alterations of the footpath between the two Mills on the next two pages. Followed by illustration based on 1906 map.

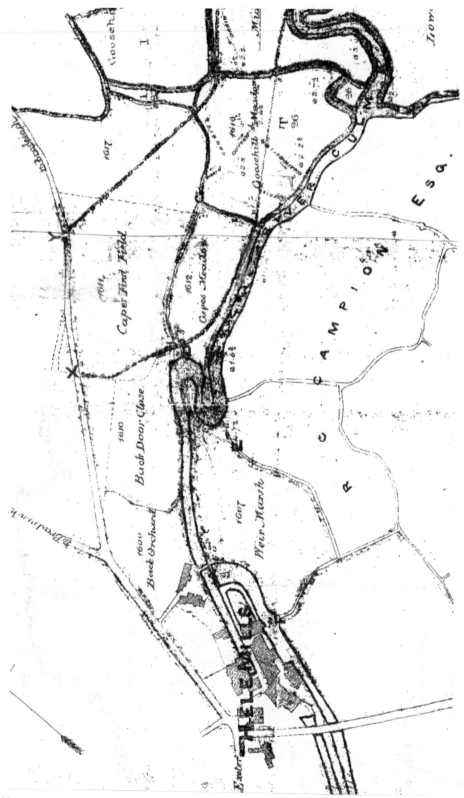

62

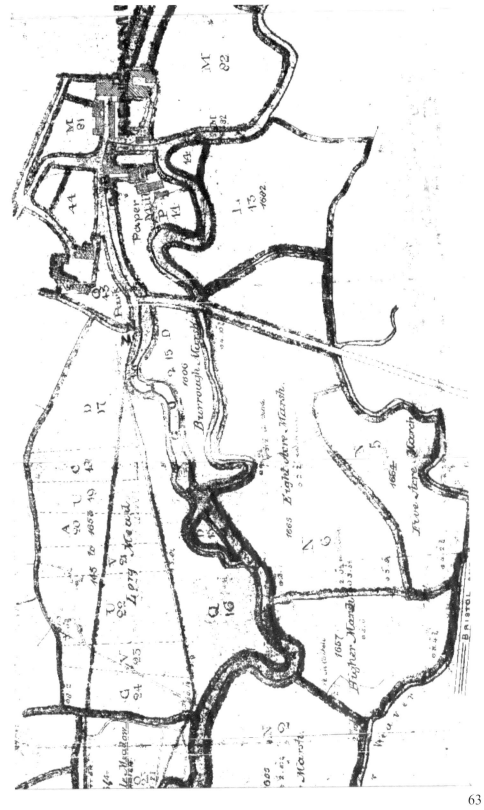

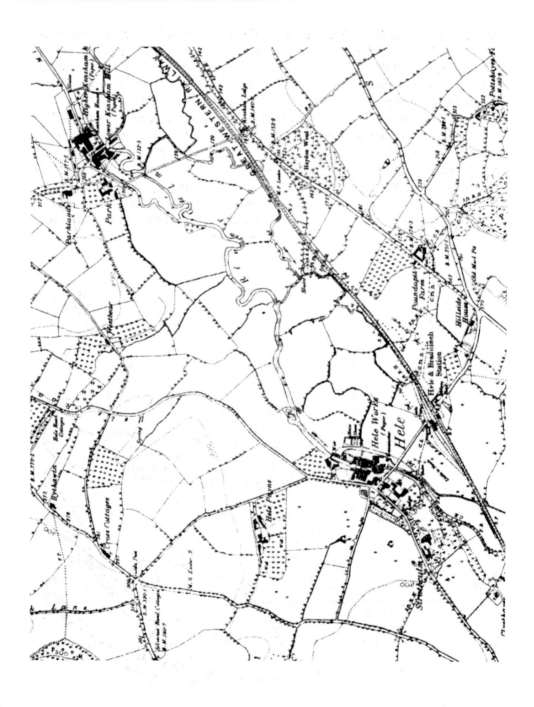

KENSHAM MILLS, BRADNINCH – PLANS OF THE TWO PAPER MILLS.

Separate and distinct from Hele Mill and Hele, Kensham Mills were situated down on the river Culm below the town of Bradninch. They were therefore very involved and part of the history of that town. It was also part of the paper-making industry along the river Culm so worth including in this book on Hele a few plans of those Mills and Mill Houses to see similarities and differences.

Kensham Mills produced paper throughout the nineteenth century so there would have been some interaction between them and Hele Mills. Kensham Mills was successful but lacked the direct link to the railway network from the middle of that century, which aided Hele's expansion and success. Kensham Mills may have had a longer history, but maybe they were also more tied into the past of the town. There was certainly enough business and workers for the two paper mills – Higher and Lower Kensham – and a fine house of the nineteenth century from an earlier dwelling illustrated the high standing of the owners.

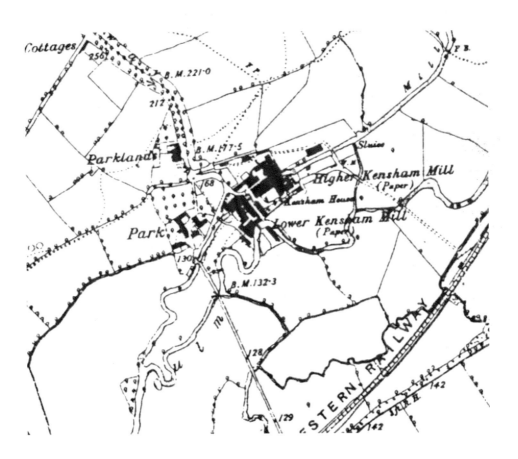

The illustration above of an early twentieth century map give clear layout of the two Mills at Kensham. On the three following pages are illustrations of plans of the Higher and Lower Mills there; also the garden view of Kensham House in occupation.

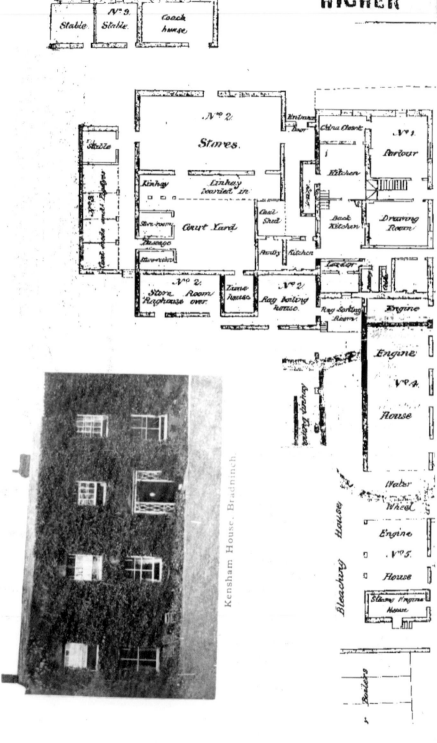

Stable

N° 3. Stable

Coach house

N° 2

Stores

Skittle

Linhay

Linhay carted in

Store-room

Passage

Storeroom

Court Yard

Coal Shed

Entrance Door

China Closet

Kitchen

N° 1

Parlour

Back Kitchen

Drawing Room

N° 2

Store Room Raghouse over.

Lime house

N° 2

Rag boiling house

Larder

Rag Sorting Room

Engine

Engine

N° 4.

House

Bleaching House

Water Wheel

Engine

N° 5.

House

Steam Engine House

Boilers

Kensham House, Bradninch.

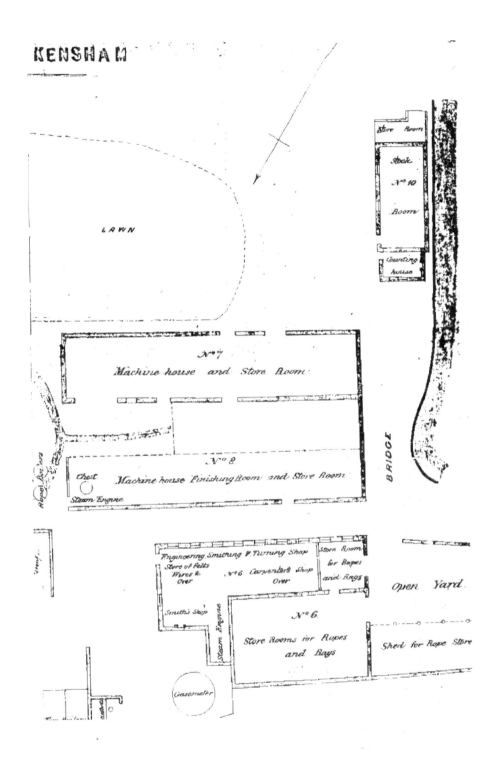

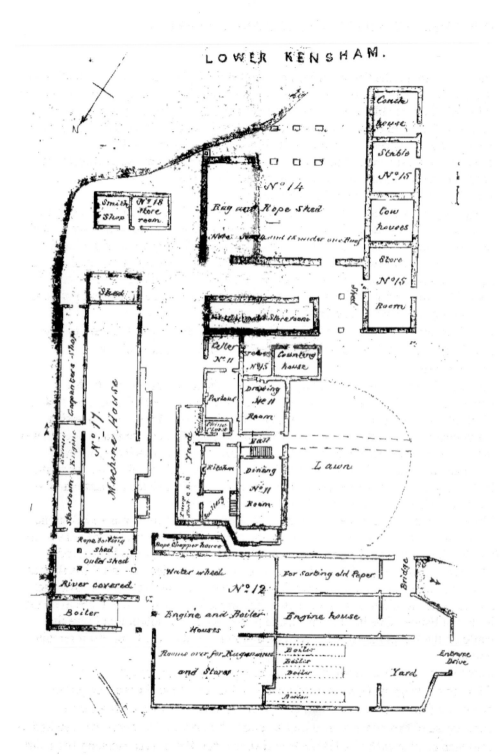

LOWER KENSHAM.

THE RIVER CULM BETWEEN HELE AND KILLERTON.

The river through the Culm Valley has flooded throughout known time, but it was also the life supply for communities that developed along its length from the source in the Blackdown Hills to its joining the river Exe. That larger river took the waters of the Culm out to sea. The Paper Mill at Hele developed on the river and expanded with success. It probably also polluted the water that flowed downstream westwards. The Mill's involvement on the river was to control the flow into the Mill from the eastern upstream and on the western downstream side to make sure the water flowed quickly away.

A legal agreement between John Dewdney of Heale Mills and Sir Thomas Dyke Acland of Killerton dated March 17th 1843 attempted to resolve an answer to that second problem for the Mill. A map attached to the deed gave details of land ownership; it also detailed the extensive work to be carried out to satisfy the agricultural needs of the tenant farmers on the fields along the river that were owned by Acland but which also gave Dewdney relief from his pressing problem of flooding in the Mill. The deed states –

'Jno. Dewdney had lately with the consent and partly at the expense of the said Thos. Dyke Acland altered the ancient and cut a new drain or watercourse.'

There could have been a secondary reason why those two men came to that agreement. The River Culm passed unhindered through the Mill with water taken off it into the works, used, then returned to the river east of the Mill, through a water channel called the Mill Leat. There could have been an ongoing dispute over the polluting of the river Culm by the paper manufacturer, which may have adversely affected Acland's fields and water that the cattle drank. The weir with its fenders and hatches (marked E on the map) was built to keep the Leat and the river thereafter at a lower level than the preceding river.

The new watercourse started from the river just above the weir (marked B on the map) and so drew away good clean river water that had not been mixed with water that had been through the Paper Mill. That watercourse, or as it is known today 'the river across the fields' had fenders and hatches installed to control the flow at that point, and then ran through the fields parallel with the river for approximately a mile before it rejoined the river before Silverton Mills, which was close in on the Killerton Estate. One has to leave aside that although the solution did give the cattle on the Acland Estate clean drinking water, it did let the Culm itself remain polluted.

There were some interesting details incorporated in the document.

'That said Sir Thos. Dyke Acland should not at any time thereafter put or place any fender or cause any impediment to the free flow of the water through said watercourse at a higher point than where the same was marked in said map or plan with the letter H and where for the better marking the point on said land 2 bond stones were to be placed but that below such point said Sir Thos. Dyke Acland should have full liberty by fender or otherwise to throw said water over the adjoining lands for all purposes whatsoever at his and their will and pleasure.'

'That said Sir Thos.Dyke Acland should not at any time thereafter make or allow to be made any channel or gutter for the purpose of throwing any of the water from said new watercourse into the river higher up said river than the lower end of a field called the Great Puddy Marsh at the point marked L in said map ... and that Sir Thos. Dyke Acland should at all times thereafter keep the banks of his land between said point marked K and the lands of the said John Dewdney to a level of a Stone then placed by the side of said river in a line with said bond stones marked H ... should not at any time thereafter lower the banks of the river adjoining his land as they then stood between said point marked K and said point L ... and this said watercourse should for ever thereafter be continued of the size and width and of the shape described.'

There does seem to have been a great deal of thought taken to prevent the Mill from suffering flooding; the new watercourse was to be the channel to speed up the flow of flood water in winter from the Mill area.

'That during the Summer months (that is to say) from 1st April to the 1st October in every year said John Dewdney his heirs or assigns should .... keep open the fenders or hatches marked E in said map so as to cause the water proceeding from said weir to run into the river at that point and should also shut down said fenders or hatches marked B during the same period..... so as to exclude the said water from passing into said lands of said Sir Thos. Dyke Acland.'

'That during the Winter months (that is to say) from the 1st October in every year .... to the 1st April .... shut down said fenders or hatches marked E and keep open said fenders or hatches marked B in order that said water might run into and through said new watercourse...'

'...but if at any time by reason of said Jno.Dewdney Mills being partially or entirely stopped a larger supply of water than usual should be thrown over the weir marked A and there should consequently be a larger stream than usual in said watercourse between said weir and said fenders marked B then said John Dewdney should wholly or partially open said fenders marked E in order to stop a larger stream than usual from passing through said fenders marked B and to rush of water on and over the land of said Sir Thos. Dyke Acland.'

Twenty years later a hand written letter dated 25th October '77 gives us insight into the continuing difficulties in the meadows. It was from Charles Collins the then owner of the Mill, following on from Dewdney. He made a great success of papermaking, he built a fine house, Strathculm, in Hele and became a landed gentleman. The letter was to Sir T D Acland Bart. M.P., the son of the Sir Thomas Dyke Acland who had signed the 1843 document.

' Dear Sir Thomas,   My Solicitor, Mr Drake, gave me a letter yesterday which he had from Mr Follett asking me, on your behalf, if I should make some alteration in the deed of agreement made on 17th. March 1843 between your Father and Mr. Dewdney respecting the water on the meadows during the winter months, but did not say what the proposal was –

I told Mr. Drake to reply and say how happy I will be to do anything I can to meet your wishes in anyway, so that the rights of my Factory are not interfered with. Could we not talk it over rather than take this seemingly roundabout way of through our Solicitors who neither of them I suppose know anything of the practical workings of the matter. I shall be happy to call on you if you can name a time when you will be home. Yours faithfully, C R Collins '

A few modifications were added to the original document in October 1877 so one assumes a successful outcome of the interchange. Those were

' 1) That at any time during the Winter Months the fender or hatches at E shall be lifted at his request [Sir Thos. Acland] so far as it may be possible without water logging the Mill. 2) At point K the 15inch fender is inserted within a larger fender of twice the size – Sir Thomas desires in times of flood to be allowed to lift the larger fender. 3) To be allowed in draining the land chequered on the plan if he finds it desirable to do so, to carry this water into the river at a point above L.

The object of these modifications is to carry the water from the meadow now frequently flooded and materially damaged.'

Whether in the 1870's there was just more flooding of the Culm Valley at Hele that caused this situation of 'material damage' or whether the constructions and alterations of the natural river line and flow caused more flooding problems in the water meadows cannot easily be ascertained a century or more later.

An exploration of the water meadows revealed several of those man-made features of the watercourse construction; some have disappeared, others are faint ruins in the landscape. The laying of the Railway across that flood plain had added other features some of which again lay half hidden in the ground. [A diagram map following shows them as of today.]

Most permanent and very much as it was laid out is the 'new watercourse' itself. It is a beautiful stream with wild plants such as reeds and tansy along its banks, and except in a few places, are not broken down by cattle. The exception being at D where it has become a drinking and fording place.

The footbridge across the watercourse is further downstream than on the original plan as, in living memory, a concrete one strong enough to take a tractor has replaced the old wooden one. (marked 2 on map)

There was a hard search for the Marker Stones but the place at H was discovered. The banks had been reinforced with large boulders that have fallen into the stream, some ending up downstream by the force of winter floods; but there could be seen a large cut-shaped stone in one bank, and possibly the other one, although more hidden, on the other side. It was a drought summer in 2003 and the watercourse was so shallow a wooden beam and stumps of a structure were exposed going across the watercourse at that point. Referring back to the original document about the rights granted, it would seem to be the remains of a fender fitted into the watercourse at that important position and the most easterly point for Sir Acland to control the water flow.

Keeping to the watercourse there has been seen in this and other dry summers the wooden stumps of the original Railway Bridge as laid down by Brunel. They are the only remains of about eight large posts, in a line across the watercourse under the present bridge. The original bridge must have been demolished at the time of its replacement but the old wooden supports cut off just above the river bed have survived in gentle decay, as with the fender at H, preserved in water and only rarely exposed to the air. (marked C on map)

Moving over to the river Culm itself there should have been a Marker Stone on the riverbank in line with the two at site H on the watercourse.   The bank and field along that length of the river was overgrown and so needed an exploration in the winter months. (marked 3 on map)

Proceeding down stream the site at K was found. The culvert from D to K and on into the river was totally dry, and around K and to the river it was very overgrown even to large willows that had fallen and were re-growing. The fender that the later Sir Acland in 1877 requested to enlarge from 15inches to fit in one twice the size has totally gone. What is still there and what makes such an attractive area was the stone constructed semi-circular water tunnel of about 30 inches height at K.

Across the top and with side kerbing is a stone bridge wide enough so that a cart would have been able to cross there even when the culvert was flowing full.

Half way between K and site no.3 there was marked on the ordnance survey map an Aqueduct across the River Culm. It is no longer there but there was within living memory an iron box shaped girder across the river at that place.   It was very rusty and dangerous as there was no top surface on it and the base was almost totally rusted through so that crossing meant stepping carefully on any remaining cross members. Children of course loved it. Today the large stone base that was built into the bank on the field side to support the Aqueduct is still there. The original purpose of it remains a puzzle, why take water across a river? and what water? as there is no sign of any pipe-work to this structure. Maybe the river Culm was so polluted for cattle to drink that somehow water was moved from the watercourse to the field on the other side of the Culm. If there had been no pipe, water would only flow across during flood times; rather pointless as at those times there would have been water over the land both sides of the river.

Two other features made at the time of the construction of the watercourse across the meadow in the nineteenth century remain in some degree in the landscape today. First there is a ridge of hard stony earth, now smothered in wild plants and grass, which it is assumed is of the soil that was excavated in the making of the watercourse.   It runs down the field from the weir end (between points marked E and B on the map) following the line of the Culm river almost to the end of the present field at the railway bridge opposite Clyst Hayes. (marked 4 on the map)   It is a very useful causeway for people and animals and as an escape area and way out of the field when the floods cover the area. It remains high and slightly dry except for the very highest floods when even that disappears under rushing water.

It may have been put there not only to get rid of that excess soil but also to create a barrier between the water in the Culm and the meadow water in times of flood. The second feature (marked 5 on the map) was a shallow earthen channel parallel alongside the raised ridge starting half way down from the weir end and in the centre of the field. It led to the centre railway bridge in that field. That bridge was built to span a wide flood channel. Just next to it can be found an earlier flood tunnel; circular, brick-built, about three foot in diameter. Obviously that turned out not to be big enough to carry the flood-water from that first field, under the railway, to the other field beyond. On the other side and leading from it there were remains of another shallow channel (marked 6 on the map). That went westward towards the River Culm beyond the railway bridge that is opposite Clyst Hayes. The central part of this where it bends at an angle near the railway embankment can still be seen; the floor and both sides constructed of stone. It looks as if it was only that part so built with the rest as an earth channel. Now of course all the earth channels are grassed but show in the fields by the lush grass and mixture of wild plant including rushes within them because the channel or what we would describe today as a depression holds water longer throughout the spring into summer. The stone lined section could be suggested to have been a sheep dip in the distant past but no recollection of that activity there has been found.

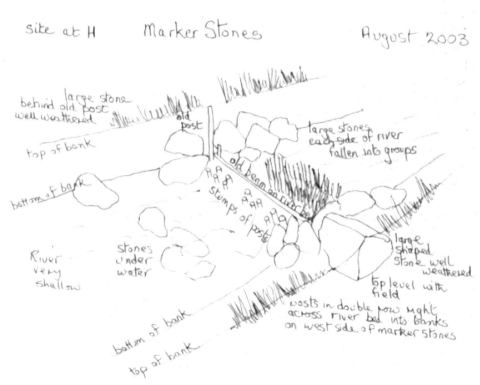

Above – Sketch plan of the Marker Stone and timber remains of Fender below water in the watercourse at site H.

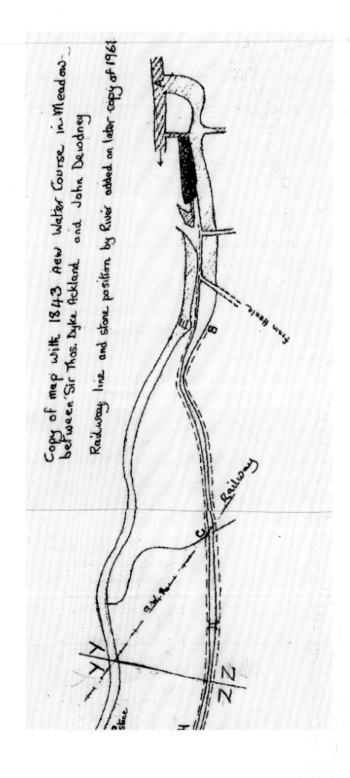

Copy of map with 1843 new Water Course in Meadows
between Sir Thos. Dyke Ackland and John Dewdney

Railway line and stone position by River added on later copy of 1961

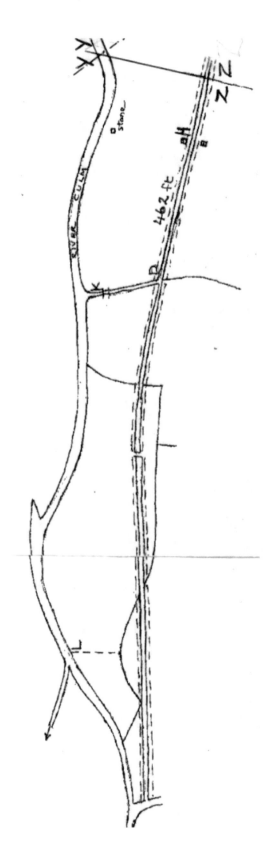

Illustration of a copy of the 1843 Map of the New Watercourse in the meadows. The railway line and stone position by the River Culm added in pencil later in 1961. The Hele Mill is shown top of first page and the second page follows on down river from the first page to the point of rejoin of the watercourse to the river.

Two illustrations of the rebuilding of the Weir in the early 1950's. It was called the Sluice Bridge, with hatches and gearing to control the water flow between the Culm and the river across the fields, west of the Mill. Top view – from the field looking across the building work; in background is The Drive area to Station Road bridge and the Mill. Bottom view – the opposite view; from the end of The Drive showing the structure and towards the field to the west. The Weir was demolished in the 1980's, it being considered no longer needed; the River Authority keen to remove obstructions to the natural flow of the river.

76

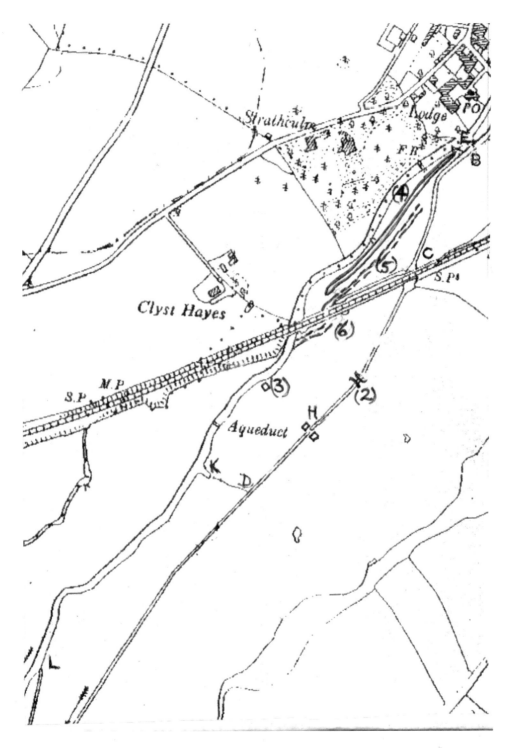

Above: Illustration map showing features in the landscape in 200
Aqueduct – The solution to the puzzle of the purpose of that feature came to light from Bob
Gitsham when he talked to me of his early life in Hele. I have not transferred the
information to this item as it can be read in his memories item – Kicking About in Hele,
Page 155.

Below is an illustration of the Watercolour Painting of the Paper Mill and Station Road Bridge from the west. It was painted in 1954 by Mr.Cartwright, who was a travelling artist. This painting is owned by Robert Gitsham and reproduced here with his permission; This is a black and white tonal copy. A different Watercolour by Mr.Cartwright was featured in the first book 'Memories from the Mill', page 110, and described on page 97.

THE VISIT OF H.R.H. PRINCE GEORGE TO HELE MILLS IN 1931.

A report in THE PAPERMAKER AND BRITISH PAPER TRADE JOURNAL of July 1st. 1931 describes the visit of Prince George to Hele Mills on the 25th June of that year.

'While in the West Country Prince George also visited that very charming spot, Bradninch, and beneath the shady trees on the beautiful lawn of Bradninch House he shook hands with a number of Duchy tenants. As he greeted the Prince of Wales's tenants a peal of bells rang out over the valleys from the Parish Church. It was then that His Royal Highness turned from the rural to the industrial. At the paper mills of Messrs. Wiggins Teape and Co (1919) Ltd. he made a thorough inspection of the whole process of paper-making. He saw white-clad girls and women dextrously sorting hundredweights of clean linen rags and cutting them into the required lengths, and watch those same rags transformed into beautiful paper – blotting paper and ledger paper.

It was curious to watch how a pink liquid stream passing slowly over overhead rollers gradually assumed the texture and shape of blotting paper of a uniform pink colour. Elsewhere he saw scores of girls, with fingers that moved with such swiftness that they were difficult to follow, examining the paper for flaws. He saw a giant guillotine at work, and, indeed, watched every process in paper manufacture. He put scores of questions to Mr. H. M. Richardson, the manager, who was his guide, and who was accompanied by Mr. J. Horsburgh, a director, and Mr. F.W. Pirie.

In a large house nearby, which is temporarily untenanted, the Prince took a quick lunch, and within 20 minutes or so was on the road again. The girls from the factory assembled to give him a wonderful send-off.

The Prince was received at the Devon Valley paper mill at Hele, by Mr. John Horsburgh, who presented Mr. F.W. Pirie, one of the directors, deputising for Col. Wyndham R. Portal, chairman of directors, who was unavoidably detained in London, and Mr. H.M. Richardson, the mill manager. Just before 2 o'clock the Prince left Strathculm House. Mill girls lined the sides of the drive beyond the gate and cheered as the Prince's car was driven away again towards Exeter.'

The visit of the Prince to the paper mill at Hele created a great deal of thought, planning and preparation. Mr. Richardson, the Manager sent detailed instructions to all departments within the works. These were all dated 18/6/31, which was seven days prior to the visit. In general they had very similar instructions in that he informed them all:

'H.R.H. PRINCE GEORGE will visit the Mill between 12.30 and 1.30 p.m. on 25/6/31. The work of the mill will carry on as usual, but the following instructions should be noted:-- NO-ONE will leave work between 12.30 and 1.30 p.m. i.e. dinner hour for all day workers will be put back to 1.30 p.m. or later if the visit is not completed by that hour.'

To Mr. Nott

'All machinery and processes likely to be inspected should be running as far as practicable, e.g.:- Rag Washer; Machines on long runs of watermarked paper (if possible). Wires and felts to be in good order, so that a shift or breakdown of any sort is unlikely; Airdryers should be Airdrying; Broke Pulper.

On no account will a Drum of Chlorine be turned on until 2.15 p.m. or later if the visit is later.'

To Mr. Ewart

'No work likely to impede the progress of the inspection will be carried out during the time of the visit. No work will be done at Strathculm on that day. Arrange for Dart to be free on that day, i.e. on night shift.'

To Mr. Tett

'The machinery and processes likely to be inspected should be running as far as practicable, e.g.:- Cutters (and perhaps Slitter if convenient); Guillotines; Ripple or Linen Finishing; Press Baling, (if possible Bales should be arranged to show the various Colonies to which we export); A Container should be loading; Stacking Machine should be working; Higher way to be kept clear, and Blotting folding to be in the Salle.'

To Mr. Carpenter

'All machinery will be running during the visit, i.e. a Boiler will be filling. All the women should wear clean overalls and caps.'

To Mr. F. Miller

'You will hoist the new Union Jack from the Rosin House, and the Red Ensign from the Airdryer pole, and they will be flown all day, i.e. 8 a.m till 5 p.m.

The Yard will be kept clear for the Royal party, which will consist of 3 cars, led by a Motor Cycle and followed by a Motor Cycle. The cars will come in and turn while the Mill is being inspected, and will wait in the Mill Yard until the visit over.

On no account may ANYONE, with exception of the Royal Cars, enter the Mill between 12.30 and 1.30 p.m. or later if the visit is not over by 1.30 p.m. This applies to TRAVELLERS ETC. AND TO ALL PRESS PHOTOGRAPHERS AND REPORTERS, with exception of any who may have official permits.

There will be Police present at the Mill entrance, and there should, therefore, be no necessity to shut the Mill Gates during the visit.'

To Mr. F. Lucas

'No one leaving work between 12.30 and 1.30 p.m. applies to horsemen and all day workers. See that no unauthorised persons come into the Mill by way of the Siding. Make certain that the Mill Yard is clear for the entrance of 3 cars and 2 Motor Cyclists at 12.12 p.m. and keep the Yard in front of the Offices quite clear until the Cars have left.

See that Siding between Turbine House and Bleach-making House is sufficiently clear for the Royal party to walk past.'

To Mr. & Mrs. Dart

'Lunch will be at Strathculm. Please note the following:-

Messrs. Palmer & Edwards of Exeter are providing all food, furniture, waiters, cooking utensils. The Red House will provide flowers, vases and cloakroom requisites.

Please arrange to be at Strathculm not later than 10 a.m. at which hour Palmer & Edwards' van will arrive. The main gates should be opened at 12.15 p.m. and closed as soon as the Cars have come in. They should be opened again to allow the Cars to leave. The back gates will be used by Palmer & Edwards' van but will be closed except when actually in use for this purpose. All the food will be cold, and Palmer & Edwards will bring a stove for heating coffee, and hot water for Clock Room. Please arrange for soap and towels for the Chauffeurs. On no account may any unauthorised person enter Strathculm House or grounds at any time during the day. This particularly applies to Press Photographers and Reporters. No work will be done in the house during that day by Nicks's men or any other decorator.'

It is assumed that the individuals named were in charge of the individual departments on that day. Mr. Nott in the most important papermaking Machine Shop; Mr. Ewart in charge of the outside workers, as he had to allow Mr. Dart to be released from night shift, maybe as a night-watchman: Mr. Tett in the Finishing and Loading departments; Mr. Carpenter in the Rag room and mixing department; Mr. Miller who was the Lodge Man and Mr. Lucas as the Yard Man.

There is a small handwritten note of a telephone message that came in to the Mill on the morning of the visit at 9. 25 a.m. which must have gone some way to relieve Mr. Horsburgh's last minute concerns as to all the final details for a smooth visit. A letter had been sent the day before to the Prince's aide, Major McCormick, to the Palace Hotel in Torquay informing that the Chairman was unable to attend and as he would have been the person to receive the Prince this must have caused a worry to the Mill Management. It reads as follows:

'For Mr. Horsburgh, Phone Message 9.25 a.m.

In reply to your letter, Major McCormack will present you to the Prince. You will thereafter please present the others'.

Among Mr. Horsburgh's handwritten notes that he made to help him through the Prince's visit were lists of the Employees with long service, with the date they commenced with the mill. Presumably he could have informed the Prince about employees as the tour progressed. The lists are as follows:

'Men with long service' were; Frank Miller 6th May 1895; James Vicary 27th June 1892; W.R.Rookes 11th July 1898; Fred Burrows 1st July 1896; W.R.Bowden 5th August 1897; Wm. John Fry 9th October1899; F.W.J.Heal 9th October 1899; Frank Leigh 29th July 1897; Wm. John Pollard 9th May 1898; Walter Sanders 5th April 1898; Wm. Henry Stark 26th June 1898.

'Women with long service' were; in the Rag Room were Harriet Jordan 24th May 1902; Dora R. Glanville 28th March 1910; and in the Salle were Alice Bussell 10th May 1910; Cora Colwill 10th May 1881; Edith Force 10th May 1892; Eliza Jane Haydon 8th January 1903.

He had a typed list of four men with service in the forces. Most likely they were in the First World War of 1914-18 and returned to the Mill, or more poignantly they were past employees killed in that war. They were:-

'E. Pearce, a Beaterman in the Mill, service in R.F.A .in France and Italy;

A. Haydon, a Beaterman in the Mill, service in R.F.A. in Afghanistan;

S. Heal, worked on Machine in the Mill, service in R.G.A. in France;

A. Bryant, worked in Breakers in the Mill, service in Devon Reg.in France.'

Illustrated below is the signature of H R H Prince George. Below his signature were those of two people accompanying him. Prince George's signature was further along in the same Visitor's Book of the Mill that the Prince of Wales signed in 1921. (illustrated on page17).

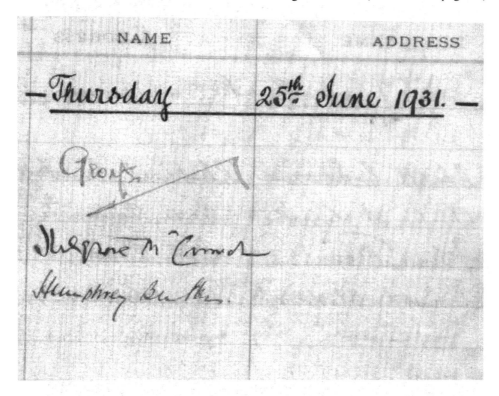

The illustration following is of the Devon Valley Staff in 1930
Back row, left to right: T. Perryman, C.E.Blackford, Miss E.E.Madge, Miss L.M.Jeffery, Miss L.M.Wingrove, Miss K.Stephens, Miss P.Passmore, Mrs I.M.Rutley,
A.L.Glanville, A.Carpenter,   Front row: J.Squire, F.Tett, W.H.Passmore,
H.M.Richardson, C.G.Nott, J.Ewart, C.H.Churchill.

The very fine leather-bound Visitors Book was started in June 1912. It started with four and a half pages of the history of the paper mill at Hele up to that date. This was written in fine handwriting headed:

'Copy of Article which appeared in the "Devon & Exeter Daily Gazette" 1st August 1893.   Devonshire Industries. Hele Paper Mill.'

Following this, the next two pages are headed with Directors, Foremen & Staff of the Hele Paper Co. Ltd. June 1912.

The name and address, position being held and date of entry into the Mill was given for each person.

Thos. H. Hepburn, Bradninch, Devon,   Chairman of the Hele Paper Co. Ltd.
1 Oct. 1873   [died 2/2/17] (in brackets in different handwriting)
John Horsburgh, Exeter,   Director of the Hele Paper Co. Ltd.   11 Nov.1883
J. Patrick Hepburn, Bradninch,   (Director).   11 Oct. 1897
George Bonner, The Square, Hele,   Gate Keeper,   13 Mch.1854
John Heal, Hele Square, Hele,   Yard Foreman,   1 June. 1863
Thomas Squire, Linningtons, Bradninch,   Stores Clerk,   16 Aug. 1868
J Robertson Pirie, The Laurels, Hele,   Foreman papermaker (day),

26 Jan. 1902

Benjamin Heal, Hele,   Foreman Papermaker (night),   7 Oct. 1878
P. Webster, The Bindles, Hele,   Foreman Engineer,   18 Feb. 1908
J. Ferriss, Hele,   Salle Foreman,   7 July. 1896
William John Ball, Jenkins, Bradninch,   Rag House Foreman,   2 Nov. 1898
William H. Passmore, Ringmer House, Hele,   Chief Clerk & Cashier,

6 May. 1896

C.H.Churchill, Myrtle House, Bradninch,   Sales Ledger Clerk,   24 Jan. 1900
Charles G. Nott, The Square, Hele,   Orders Clerk,   7 Nov. 1900
Frank Tett, 65 Victoria St, Exeter,   Orders Clerk,   11 Dec. 1911
Thomas Perryman, Fore Street, Bradninch,   Salle Clerk,   7 May. 1901
R. Spencer Blamey, Devonshire Cottages, Cullompton,   Salle Clerk,

13 May. 1912

F.E.Ferriss, Hele, Cullompton, Devon,   Typist,   11 May. 1903
E. Mountstephen, Parsonage Street, Bradninch,   Typist,   25 Jun. 1904
F.K.Wood, Coombe, Bradninch,   Sample Clerk,   10 Aug. 1907

(each item was written in by each individual person and a few of the letters are more difficult to be certain of than others but on the whole they are very legible.)

The details in the list in the Visitors Book give some good facts of the working within the Mill at that time and firm facts on names and dates. Of interest is the prominent position in the list of the Foremen of the different working departments. The individual employees can sometimes be linked to other items of information.

To take the longest in employment in the mill first.

George Bonner, the Gatekeeper had worked for 58 years by 1912, and if he entered at an early age of say 14, would have been born in 1840.

John Heal, the Yard Foreman, appears on the 1901 census aged 48 so was born in 1853. If it is the same John Heal as on the list in 1912 he would then have been aged 59 with 49 years of service. He would have been 10 years old when he started in 1863.

To remain in the same family, Benjamin Heal the Foreman Papermaker, is on the 1901 census as aged 35 so was born in1864. On the 1912 list he would have been aged 46 with 34 years of service. He therefore entered the mill in 1878 aged 12.

To move on to four other employees.

Charles G.Nott, the Orders Clerk on the 1912 list entered the mill in 1900. On the 1901 census there was a Robert Nott, papermaker, living in Hele. He was aged 47, with wife and four children. The third child was a son, Charles, aged 14 and listed as Boy in Paper Mill, who, if the same person, made him 25 years of age in 1912 and the Orders Clerk. The second interesting fact about him is that he could have been in the Staff photograph of 1930. [illustration prior this item, page 83] A Mr. C.G.Nott is seated in the front row next to Mr. Richardson. If so, he was then aged 43, and in a very responsible job. Also following this it would seem most likely that he was the Mr Nott who was in charge of the paper machine when Prince George visited in 1931 one year later and had been given instructions by Mr. Richardson, the Manager. [ref. previous item, page 79]

Frank Tett is the second man also linked forward to the Prince George visit. He was in the Mill as an Orders Clerk, and started in 1911. In the 1930 Staff photograph there is an F.Tett seated also in the front row, and in 1931 Mr. Richardson's instructions for the royal visit goes also to a Mr.Tett who was obviously in charge of the Finishing Room and Salle. He would have been about 35 years of age assuming he started as a young employee. [ref. item, page 79]

J Robertson Pirie in the 1912 list may have had links within the Mill. He was listed as Foreman Papermaker although only joining Hele Mills ten years earlier. In the newspaper reports of the Prince's visit in 1931 there was mention of a Mr.F.W. Pirie, a Director, who was deputising for the Chairman of Directors, and who, with others, accompanied the Prince around the Mill. The surname Pirie is uncommon so there may have been a family link between the two over 19 years. [ref. item, page 79]

C.H.Churchill, the Sale Ledger Clerk of 1912, could have been related to Charles Churchill listed in the 1901 Census, aged 28 and living in Hele, and listed as a Papermaker. Charles Churchill would have been 39 in 1912 and could have been the Sale Ledger Clerk's father. C.H.Churchill is in the 1930 Staff photograph.

Two other names on the 1912 list also occurred on the 1901 Census.

J. Ferris, the Salle Foreman, who had started in the Mill in 1896 could have been the John Ferris listed on the 1901 Census, aged 41, living in Hele Square, and who was described as a Papermaker Finisher. The Salle was the finishing workshop. John Ferris from the census would have been born in 1860 and by 1912 would

have been 52 and the right age to hold that Foreman position. On the same 1912 list was an F.E.Ferris, a typist, who had started in the Mill in 1903. On the 1901 Census, in the household of John Ferris, was listed his wife and eldest daughter, Florence, aged 11. If Florence was the same person as F.E.Ferris she would have started work in the Mill aged 13 and been 22 at the time of the 1912 list.
F.K.Wood, the Sample Clerk of 1912 could have been related to a William Wood listed in the 1901 Census, aged 45 and listed as a Garden Labourer and who lived on Cullompton Hill in Bradninch. William Wood would have been born in 1856 and so could have been the father of F.K. Wood. Another link is the agricultural one, as F.K. Wood lived at Coombe in 1912 which is a farming area of Bradninch.

Other facts emerge from these formal lists and events.
First there is the inclusion of the later pencilled insertion of the date 2/2/17 of the death of Thos. H. Hepburn. From other sources it is known that he was born in 1841, so he entered the Mill aged 32, and died aged 76. For the family and also to some extent the family business at the paper mill the year 1917 must have been especially traumatic because in 1917, the younger son was killed in the First World War. A fine memorial plaque in the Baptist Church in Bradninch, and a set of three stain glass windows in the Porch were erected to his memory. The family home was at Dunmore, a fine large house, in Bradninch. The family was well placed with wide influences in the town. [ref. fuller detail of Roger are in a separate item 'The Chestnut Tree in the Centre of Hele Square' page 100]
John Patrick Hepburn, the elder son, was involved in the running of the business and was living at The Red House in Hele, but for him also the year 1917 must have caused practical as well as emotional changes in his life. He had been born about 1880 and had entered the Mill quite young in 1897 and spent all of his working life there. He married in June 1912 to Rose Marion Tosswill and they had three daughters. He was known as Patrick Hepburn, and as 'Mr. Pat' by some of the workforce. With the loss of his father, John Patrick Hepburn became the head of the extended family with a widowed mother, two sisters unmarried, and the younger brother killed.
John Horsburgh, the other Director of the Company, was the son in law of Thos. H. Hepburn. He married Alice Frances Hepburn, the third daughter, in September 1910, and they were living at Strathculm in Hele in 1917, and had two sons.

One other name on the 1912 list raises interest; but this is the house name of P. Webster, the Foreman Engineer from 1908 to1919, who lived at 'THE BINDLES,' Hele. The name 'part of Bindles Orchard' appears on the Tythe map of 1841 on a small area in the centre of Hele that still has remnants of an old orchard. There are other areas marked as orchards with one called Higher Orchard on the opposite side of Strathculm Road (and the land there does rise steeply above the road) and Fore Orchard alongside it. The name Bindles has been a puzzle in connection with Hele and was questioned in a link to the 'Puzzle of Late Warrens Land', an item in my earlier book, Memories from the Mill. More information has been found so a separate item has been written in this book on Bindle's Orchard and Late Warrens land.

A sixteen-page foolscap, closely typed document came to light.   The document
was entitled 'Notes from the Engineer's Diary 1924 –1944' with sub-title 'Twenty
years at Devon Valley Mill by John Ewart.'   He took over as Mill Engineer from
Mr.W.Y.Frew.   Most of the accounts were about the technical alterations and
maintenance of the machinery and buildings in the Mill at Hele, which are beyond
the scope of this book.   There were also items of a more general nature and some
that have relevance to items and individual memories in this book and in my first
book, Memories from the Mill.   These will be written as directly copied notes here
(with connecting references) rather than dispersed into the other relevant items.
A]   Rag room and rag rotting stores.
1927; 'First Rag Rotting Store was put into use in August. Situated on site of
old settling pit at the back of the rag-boiling house next to the wood pulp
store. Later extensions constructed until all the area which was garden,
between wood pulp store and the road to Venmans was taken to form rotting
stores and roofed over.'
1928; 'A 16inch wide conveyor belt was installed to take dusted and cut rags
from the delivery end of the top duster and deliver them to the boilers.   This
was in commission on 5th March. This conveyor was a great success, much more
so than an attempt some years ago to blow the rags into the boilers; it also cut
out the laborious and slow method of catching the rags in baskets, trundling
them along the floor to the boilers and tipping them through the door.'
1930; 'A row of laburnum and lilac trees planted along road against the rag-
rotting stores.'
1936; 'New arrangement of benches in Rag Room. Improvement that the dust
was drawn from under the benches instead of from above making more
comfort for the workers.'   Other item linked: first book; page 19.
B]   Water Divining.
1927; 'In November Water Diviners Mullins and Beavis traversed the Mill
lands but no steps were taken to develop their findings'.
                                        Other item linked: this book, Wells, page 131.
C]   Mill railway siding.
1924-25; 'Mill sidings only partly formed of clinkers, flue dust and general mill
rubbish. Concrete piers built at 3 points in the meadow for bridges; bridged
openings through embankment being necessary to allow the free flow of flood
water as the meadows are liable to flooding in winter..... Bridge into Mill Yard
near the powerhouse was constructed by using two heavy second hand side
decking girders across the river in one span, with cross girders between and
to carry rails. Rails throughout were second hand flat bottom type purchased
from G.W.R. and laid from the railway gate to the Mill by Mill men, who were
working short time due to slackness of trade. S. Denmead, one of the G.W.R.

packers was borrowed and for a time acted as ganger when connecting up and laying the line over part of the distance to the Mill ..... First loaded truck of coal to pass over the line was pushed along by manual labour on the 31st January 1925, truck no. 'Ocean 6476', a great event this as it foreshadowed the stoppage of all (or most) road traffic (of raw materials at least) between the Station and the Mill.'   Other item linked: this book, Floods, page 140.

D]   Tractor.

1938; 'Allis Chalmers tractor tried out on the sidings for truck haulage – proved successful and one was purchased.' item linked: first book; Horses, page 69

Engineering and building improvements.

1926; 'New 40 ton Railway weighbridge made by Ashworth was installed on the siding for weighing the outgoing and incoming trucks.'

1930; 'New private telephone system installed throughout the Mill linking all departments.   9th May in commission.'

1935; 'The building to house Humidifier is 132'-6" long; 48' wide; 13'-6" high. The site is below the weir at north end of Mill. The lip of weir raised first and dam across river below site to prevent river overflowing into excavations. June 1935 was exceptional in Devon as far as rainfall was concerned and during this month the river rose on four occasions to an abnormal height, overflowing its banks and the heightened weir and dam completely submerging all the work which had been done previously, carrying away nearly all the shuttering, scaffolding etc; the contractor just being in the 'nick' of time to re-enforce the platforms carrying the portable pumping plant.....This flooding caused considerable delay, as the whole area had to be pumped out before work could be again started and an idea of what this entailed can be imagined when it is remembered that the river at this site is approximately 70 feet wide..... On the occasion of the first pumping out of the river bed after the dam was put in, the night shift workers were so keen on having eels, dace etc. which could be caught as the river level was lowered by the pumps, that some of them did not go home until well on in the afternoon of the same day, but to their credit it must be stated that a promise given to the Manager – an enthusiastic fisher – was fulfilled to the letter in that all trout caught were returned to the river.'

1935; 'Sample room built on river bank adjacent to Sallle foreman's office. Laboratory built next to Papermaker's office for testing paper.'

1937; 'New guillotine (Victory Kidder) installed in place of 2 old ones (Greig).'

1938; 'Engineer's office and store moved to back of General Offices, which had been a house (Mr. Quant's). He had retired and gone to Bradninch.' 'Trailer Fire Pump installed (part of fire fighting equipment). House built next to ambulance room in October. Old manual fire pump house converted into up to date ambulance and first aid room – opposite side of main gate from the

Lodge.'

1939; 'New 20 ton Ashworth weighbridge installed at Mill gate on site of old 6 ton machine.' 'R.D.C. mains water supply to corner house (Dart's).' [Mews Cottage] '...and to Ringmere. Strathculm reservoir connected and storage tank installed in Clematis Bungalow with distributing pipe lines to back of houses in Hele Square, service taps in each yard and toilets connected. Red House connected to R.D.C. mains water.'

1940; '21st January. Severe weather frost 29 degrees. Sprinkler pipes burst all over the Mill, fine spray (in Rag Room it was freezing so it froze as it fell). All radiators in Rag Room burst.'

1943; 'Corner house, now Eveleigh's (late Dart) wired for electric lights and heating. September 8th.'

Production information.

1925; "Dimpled' paper was made for the first time on No.1 Machine.'

1927; 'Start of packing and into bales for export market at Mill. Previously paper sent to London to be packed into cases or crates. Special Dept. built at Hele for this.'

1936; 'Considerable amount of paper stored in Stock Room on racks. Total in stock for year 830 tons, loaded directly into trucks under covered way, shunted to siding for G.W.R. distribution.'

Personnel information.

1924; at start of notes: 'J.P.Hepburn and J.Horsburgh are resident Directors; A.W. Pirie acting as their assistant. Richardson is Mill Manager.
Other items linked: this book, Prince of Wales, page 13, Prince George, page 79, Visitors Book, page 84.

1927; 'Mr. Pirie left to go to Aldgate (London). G.B.C.Johnson took his place at Hele and later became a Director (sales).'

1928; '28th June a man – Wellington – lost thumb of left hand on the small guillotine by the knife overrunning.'

1938; 'Mr. Churchill retired, 65, after 38 years in the General Office.'

1939; 'War declared. W. Fry and W. Pepperell ret. started work in retirement due to younger men going. M. Nott first to go to Arsenal.' 'Workman Salter, engineer's staff, in Navy. Survived sinking of Aircraft Carrier, Courageous, also survived sinking of The Prince of Wales.'

1941; 'more men going to war work, W.Mortimore, J. Mills, J. Norman, of engineering staff.'

1942; 'three more left for war work, L.Turner, B Pring (apprentice), A.W.J. Andess, from engineer's dept.'

1943; 'H Stark completed 50 yrs in mechanics shop. Presented with a clock. 29th July by Richardson. Retirement day for Ewart (myself) but kept on like other older men due to war and lack of younger men. 65 on August 20th.'

War information.

1938; 'Former Engineer's office now warden's Post. Lectures on A.R.P. started.'

1939; 'Blackout of mill completed by 1st September.'

1940; 'Aug. 23rd a Jerry plane passed over Mill on a very low altitude; 3.30 pm. Several bombs dropped in second meadow from cattle market but clear of G.W.R. line made a racket but no damage. Bombs 'Soreamer type', 10 or 11 found later and cleared away. Aug. 28th Jerry was busy all around Exeter. Flares and bombs nearest to us west side of Sunnyside Bridge, G.W.R. line, Wellington Farm and Penstone Farm.'

1941; 'Some munitions made at Mill, not much through lack of men. Running full time over some weekends. Outlook tower on top of Rag Store roof, June. Shelters built. Women started work in export dept, first one Mrs. Cox.'

1942; 'Firewatching started January 7th. May 13th shell in Mill meadow dug out by B.D.E. 'A A type' had buried into soft ground entered at angle of 10/15 degrees travelled 10 feet underground and turned back in almost a complete circle to meet its original course and line of entry.'

'Service on Radio; entry to 4th year of War, all workers stopped work and listened to it in all departments.'

Illustration above of Mr. J.E.Ewart, Mill Engineer. 1924 – 1946.

Other item linked: this book, Layout of Mill, page 18, and Prince George, page 79.

90

BORN AND BROUGHT UP IN HELE SQUARE – MEMORIES OF DORIS GLANVILLE.

I was born in 1921 while my family was living in Hele Square. My mother's name was Elizabeth and my father's name was William. Our surname was Laity and although my mother was a local girl with a maiden name of Snell, my father came from Cornwall. In his early life, in fact up until the end of the First World War in 1918, he was not connected to Hele, Devon, or any paper-mill. He had been born in Church Street in Helston in 1880 and brought up in nearby Porthleven where his own father, called Charles, had been a Groom. I do remember having holidays in Babbacombe with that grandmother so they must have lived there at some time while I was a child.

My father went into the Navy in 1897 on the ship, the Northampton, giving a slight lie as to his age as he was only seventeen at the time. He went all over the world and fought in the China War at the turn of the century and was awarded the China Medal from Queen Victoria. I developed a great interest and some knowledge from him of the world at large that existed outside the happy safe home life in Hele Square. He was clever at many hand skills including drawing and painting and music. Later I would hear him sing at concerts locally and he sang to me many songs. One I can sing happily to this day goes as follows:

> Seagull, seagull, fly away over the sea,
> Seagull, seagull, take out this message for me,
> If you see a big ship sailing over the sea,
> Tell my Daddy his little girl is waiting at home.

His time in the Navy was all before my time. He was in it during the First World War and was in the Devon and Exeter Hospital having suffered with shrapnel in his head injury. My mother and her sister Mary used to visit the hospital at that time to help and talk with the injured troops. They fell in love and were married in nineteen-nineteen.

My mother had been working at Hele Mill before they were married. She was in the Rag Room, where they sorted out the material, a lot of it from second hand clothes and rags and then they had to boil it to reduce it to its basic fibres and starch to be used as the material to produce the paper. It was used for most of the paper-making and called rag paper in those days.

They were given a house to rent in Hele as father, when he came out of hospital also went to work in the Mill. In fact mother worked all her life there until she retired when she was sixty-one. This was through necessity while we were growing up as times were happy and safe for us children but parents had to work hard and long hours to provide enough money to keep and feed the family. My father was a Night-watchman in the Mill and I remember often taking his night-time supper to him and we would walk around the buildings. He had to visit each area and when we went into the Rag Room we would hear and sometimes see a rat or two running about. They kept out of the way in the daytime, waiting for the dark to come out from the piles of old materials.

My mother earned between nineteen shillings and twenty-nine shillings a week.

She told me that some women came to the Rag Room at the Mill all the way from Silverton walking the several miles, crossed on a footpath over the field at Worth to shorten the journey. They had lace-up boots. The field was planted with strawberries. Some people went to Silverton Mill but all, wherever they worked had to walk there, or a few might have had a bike to ride. Returning home at the end of the day they still had to do a lot of work at home with families to bring up. I remember my mother hurrying out of the Mill at lunch time which was only a half hour break for her to come home and heat up some soup and make me and my father sandwiches before rushing back still eating her own lunch. My father, being on night work had to sleep in the day but also look after us children and work his garden for vegetables and such like.

I loved my childhood in The Square. The houses all seemed to be linked together around the large Chestnut tree in the middle. I had been told it had been planted in memory of the youngest son of the Hepburns of Bradninch, who had been killed in the First World War. The Hepburns had owned the Mill then and Mr. Pat Hepburn ran it. He was tall and so also was his wife who I can remember running a clothes and blanket club in the Chapel room. They were good quality things with beautiful white sheets and I still have one last blanket in a drawer upstairs today; and I am now eighty-one years of age, so that shows how well they can last. We used to pay one shilling a month for what we bought.

As I was saying, we all were friends together and I was at home in many of the houses and had several other children to play with. I had difficulty with my homework at times, especially the sums. I used to go across to Hazel's father Mr. Heal and he would joke about me appearing, saying 'Here comes Miss Laity for help with her sums', and he was always ready to help me out. My mother used to stay at nights sometimes with Mrs Heal if he was called in to work in the Mill. Later I used to stay with her, especially if he was called away because he was the Engineer and his skill was needed at another mill.

My other special friend along with Hazel, who became Hazel Rowland, was Ruby Stark who became Ruby Abrahams. We used to play all around the countryside in Hele, with one field called 'moorfield' where we would kick a ball into the stream and we would go into the allotment there and maybe we picked a few gooseberries to eat, who knows! I remember especially us three having picnics under a huge 'conker' tree that was in the middle of 'bigfield' that was opposite the large house Strathculm. My mother would mix up lemonade from the crystals into a bottle of water to make a fizzy drink for us along with sandwiches.

As a child, as well as playing in the fields and having picnics we also played hide and seek in the areas around The Square, along the river and the wooded area up Strathculm Road, opposite the Lodge that was, and still is, known as Garden Bushes. The houses in The Square had long gardens up to the Strathculm Road and down to the river. Along Hele Road it was open into the back of the Mill with gardens along the road up to the two houses called Venmans. The ground used to be covered in dust and buttons from the Rag Room. This was before they built the high brick wall along the road which enclosed the ground into the Mill. Dad called it the Wall of China.

I think my mother worked hard to look after the house. I stayed at home until I had grown up and because they did not want me to work in the Mill as it was hard work they suggested I chose between becoming a dressmaker or going into service. I chose the latter and as I had been well brought up having been taught house skills and especially cooking by my father —another skill he had learnt while in the Navy — I was soon the cook in the household I joined. After I was married during the Second World War and my husband was away in the forces, when my first child was on the way I returned to live with my parents in Hele Square.

I helped my mother in the house and there was plenty to do. There was an outbuilding in the backyard with a boiler for the washing. On Mondays I would get up very early about four o'clock to get the washing started and aimed to have it out on the line by eight o'clock, before breakfast! We had gardens running down to the Mill leat. After getting the boys breakfast I would then go off to my work in Service. Home later and lots of household work to do in the evenings.

There was water piped to that outhouse and the toilet in the yard but all other water for drinking and food preparation had to be got from the one tap in the Square, so that took up quite a lot of the day. Each house used to keep their front pavement clean and they were made of cobbles. The road itself was of boiler ash and clinkers from the Mill and with young children crawling and playing on it they came in very dirty. We were rather crowded in the small house, especially after John, my second son was born. There were only two bedrooms and a living-room and kitchen downstairs.

The houses were built partly of cob and were quite warm and the yard at the back was useful. There was a coal-house and log pile as well as the wash room for the clothes washing. We had a couple of bags of sand, these were ready in case the river flooded high into the Square and the houses. One day I was busy in the kitchen when a rat ran in from a hole in one of the sand-bags and into the kitchen dresser. I jumped onto a chair and I'm afraid to say I didn't get down until my father came in and got rid of it. It was probably sheltering from the flood water and then sensed the food I was cooking.

Roger, my first son, enjoyed himself in the Square as a small child even though it was war time. The Chapel was given over for the use of the 'Yanks', the American soldiers, some billeted and others in camps nearby. They taught him to say 'got any gum, chum'.

At that time with so many men in the forces away from working in the Mill everyone left had to work hard and often extra hours to help out in other departments. My mother was working in the Rag Room and my father continued his job as night watchman. I was living with them (as I have mentioned) as my husband was in the forces, so as I had our two lovely sons who were only toddlers, I worked in my mother's and father's house to keep the home clean and cared for. It helped my mother out quite a bit although their quiet life was full with family life again. There was only one living room downstairs and the children were there in the day and two bedrooms so that Roger had to sleep in with my parents and John in with me and my husband when he was home on leave. After the war in 1950 we were given one of the newly-built houses in Townlands.

These were the first ones on that estate along the Hele Road and were built for families that worked on the farms in the parish of Bradninch. The Mill housed most of its workers in houses that had been built by the Mill but as neither my husband nor I worked for the Mill we could not have one of their houses for ourselves. Luckily, one of the Townlands houses was rented to us from the Council.

Of course by that time things had altered very drastically for our family and it is upsetting to remember in detail the terrible accident that befell my father, but it is not something that I would want forgotten or hidden. My father was a good man and very well liked and respected. At his funeral the Church was full and we were given a lot of support by his fellow workers.

He was killed in an accident while at work in the Mill, and, as far as can be remembered back, he was the only worker for that to happen to. To go back to how it felt for me means I will describe the day as just starting out as a very normal day, in fact a good day as I went into Exeter with my young sons. We went on the train from Hele station; the one we used to call the Woolworth train; it went at twelve o'clock on a Saturday for people to spend the afternoon in there. Usually I came home on the three o'clock train, but that day I stayed to watch the army tanks going through the town. The year was 1942 and I thought the boys would be interested in the event so we stood by Sidwell Street Church, I think the force was going for embarkation to Europe.

We caught the four o'clock train home and it was strange that as I came off the platform and walked up Station Road to the Square people I knew turned away instead of their usual greeting. The Doctor was at home and he told me my Dad had had an accident and he had seen to him in the Mill but he couldn't keep him there for me to look after him, he had had to get him to the hospital as he was very bad. He said my Mother should go in that night but it became difficult to arrange as there were no ordinary trains running, only war transport trains. There was no taxi about as they were all being used by soldiers who were still camped in and about Bradninch and were going out for evening.

My Mum was very upset and a neighbour phoned the police and they commandeered the Bradninch Taxi of Mr. Crispin to take her to the hospital. The neighbour looked after the boys and we got there at half past ten in the evening. We could spend a little time with him but had to return at twelve thirty as the taxi was needed to take someone back off leave and that couldn't be cancelled. My Dad died in the night. A policeman came round to the house in the morning and said it was bad news and then told us he had gone.

The accident had happened in the morning. Dad had been asked to put in some extra hours to help in the loading of large rolls of paper onto the trucks to be taken off to the sidings for transport away. There were three men at the back of the truck and Mr. Pepperell at the front in charge of the horse. You see the trucks were pulled along the railway track that ran from the Mill out to the main lines by one of the heavy horses the Mill used. To hold in the door of the truck after it was loaded there was an iron bar that had to be lifted up into position. The three men had to lift it together and called to each other 'Up' to lift together. Disastrously this was just the sound that the horse knew to start moving forward and it did just that and

94

my poor father got caught by the iron bar straight into his chest.

There was really no saving him although the Doctor and the Hospital tried. He was only sixty-one and had come through the time in the Navy, the China War and the First World war with medals from both and then this just happened while at work so close to home.

It was very distressful following on from the accident. To start with Father's body had to be brought home; it being wartime it could not stay at the hospital in Exeter. We had no spare room, only the room we all used. There was no getting the coffin upstairs to a bedroom. I got in touch with my husband's unit as he was in the north of England and asked for him to come home on compassionate grounds but was told they didn't know if it was possible due to war situation and he was on training. O my relief, when the next morning, I saw him walking past the window coming into the house.

He managed to arrange everything, even to getting the coffin upstairs as he had been a carpenter before the war and knew how to move items about. There had to be a Coroner Court to get a death certificate and we went to that. Before that we had been given the name of a Solicitor in Exeter and my husband and I went to see him. He was very kind and took it all over and so he went also to the court and took charge of us. He sat next to me and helped me through as I had had to go and formally identify my father. Nicks, the Builders and Undertakers in Bradninch, arranged the funeral and they laid the union jack flag over the coffin.

My Mother was in great stress over this sudden accident and the Doctor wouldn't allow her back to work. In fact she could not go back until six months later due to the shock. The Solicitor claimed compensation for her and there was another Court hearing with the Management from the Mill there. Although it had been an accident they were responsible and she got four hundred pounds. When she went back to work the compensation was paid out at the rate of ten pounds a month to supplement the money she earned. We had to go to the Police Station each time to collect it and so my mother had to work all her life.

It continued each month, after she retired, working through the four hundred pound but by the time she reached the age of sixty-nine I applied for her to have the bulk of it and hopefully some interest on the money. Again I had to go back to the Court where they said she could have it but told me to tell her not to spend it all at once as it was meant to keep her for life. I felt insulted to have to stand there and be told that after what it had been given for and it made me angry to be talked down to in that way.

I still have my father's wooden Naval 'Ditty box'. Each sailor had one in my father's time in which was kept his personal things. It has a lock and key with it still. My mother had his medal for service in the China War, but it was stolen from her house a long time ago. I have got his medals from the First World war still.

I don't want to dwell on the sadness in my life because I had such a happy childhood, I was brought up by loving parents and enjoyed my time in Hele; but in talking about my life I could not slide over my father's accident and death as if it was not important. I was brought up to have love and faith and have it still and hope it has been passed on to my children and grandchildren. I never was involved with the Church, but always went to the Gospel Meetings and still go on a Wednesday afternoon.

Going back to my early adult life, I was taken on to work in the home of the Doctor in Bradninch. The Doctor was the one that was there two before Dr. Steele-Perkins. He was Dr. Miller and lived in West End Road at Earlsland House. Soon after I started I became their cook having learnt so much from my father and mother. I lived in and I liked the work. He was a good family doctor. For instance he came into the kitchen one day and asked if I could make enough for an extra mid-day meal. It was taken each day to a person living on their own in the cottages opposite and in need of support. Another time when Miss Blackmore, who also lived nearby, was dying he went across with two hot water bottles – the large one full of hot water to keep her feet warm, the small stone one with brandy in it to help her through it. A very thoughtful man!

His wife was a bit more of a tartar in the house and would sometimes listen outside the kitchen and also watch us unnoticed to see how we were working; she didn't trust us. The Doctor would say she had gone to lie down as we servants had given her a headache.

The Manager of the Mill went down to Ivybridge to become Manager there. He asked if I would like to go and be his cook. It was a beautiful house down there but I decided to stay close to home. I was very glad I did as a year later he went to Rhodesia in Africa, and I wouldn't have wanted to leave England, or have to look for another place.

Later my own employer, the Doctor, also wanted to move and he planned to go to South Africa. He said he would send me a ticket to go out and be their cook once they were settled. He came to my parents' house after he had been called into a nearby family; in fact it was to Katie Andress to tell her that her mother had died. He came in all hunched up and stood in front of our coal fire as he said he was cold and needed the African sunshine. Very sadly as he was working at his desk the next morning he just died.

I stayed on and worked for Dr. Parry, who came and took over the Practice. Also after I was married and lived at home in Hele with my two children, as it was war time, and as my husband was in the forces, I continued to be the Cook for the Doctor. I was very busy helping at home and working as well. That was not unusual in those days, everyone had to work and keep the home going as well, and look after the children. The neighbours were always there for you in difficulties and so we supported each other.

There was as I've mentioned the Heal family, with my friend Hazel, and the Stark family with my other friend Ruby. There was in the Square the Bryants, and Mrs Bryant would look after my mum while she was unwell after my Father's death while I went shopping. Mr and Mrs Pearce lived in the Square and Roger, my son loved going into see them as they had six children and always made him welcome. Roger went into the Mill after he left school and is about to retire now after thirty years. He has ended up as an Engineering Fitter and has often been on callout even during the night. That gets harder work as you get older. My other son John started work in the papermaking when he left school at sixteen. He was at the paper mill in Cullompton and became a Reelerman, but had to retire through ill health when he was about forty-six.

To go back again I recall how both boys had pocket money at the rate of one

96

penny, old money of course, for each year of their age each week. They spent that of course, but when Roger desperately wanted a toy that was in Crispin's Toy Shop window I let him work at helping me to save up for it.

At one time Tom Bond lived In Hele and he looked after the horses. He and his wife Betty moved to Cullompton eventually and their son became Outdoor Foreman in the Mill. The Passmores lived in Hele and both worked in the Office in the Mill. She was very musical and played the organ and was the daughter of Mr 'Buller' Stark and that family was good at music and also lived in Hele. There were Mr and Mrs Mann; he worked with the horses in the Mill and also up at the Cider Factory over the railway, and their daughter, Elsie, married into the Plume family.

There was Mr Tanner who had the one light in the Square on the front of his house. He used to come out each evening to light it, it being a gas lamp in those days. There was also a Mrs Hewett and Mr and Mrs Quant, and the Millers, and the Prings and the Thomas family, although some lived in what we called Lower Hele which was the Bradninch side of the Mill tucked right into the works and known by some as Venmans. Mrs Thomas lived there but then moved to the house on the corner of Strathculm Road. She had a daughter, called Grace, who remained with her mother and worked in the Mill canteen, but sadly died young of bronchitis. It all shows how close we all were and felt part of the same big family then. It also shows how sons and daughters followed fathers and mothers in working for the same Company.

There was the Pepperell family with quite a large family. His two daughters worked in the Mill offices. The Miles family lived at the Post Office in the Square. At the back they had a bakery; he had a baking oven, so there was always wonderful bread and buns close to hand. Very sadly their young son drowned in the mill leat at the bottom of their garden. We were all extra careful to keep children away from the river if it was rising or rushing though, in fact from then on at all times.

Moving out a bit from the Square I remember that there was Mr Harry Pyne who was at the first small farm opposite Westfield in Bradninch. His two sons Frank and Charlie worked with him. The farm delivered milk around Hele and early on Harry Pyne used to bring it cycling on a bike pulling a small cart behind with a churn of milk in it. Mr Pyne was getting older and needed help on the farm and I think they had to give it up.

Later Hele Payne, the larger local farm at Hele, delivered milk by pony and trap. In the war-time they used a Land Army girl for this, and I should think she must have liked her war job doing that, but maybe she had to work long hours including milking the cows first thing in the morning.

What more can I say? There are so many memories and they all show such a different and steadier way of life before and during the Second World War. Now I am in Bradninch and it is busy, except maybe for me as I cannot get around so well. I still however feel very happy with my family following after me and hope they pass on the love and faith I was given when I was young and which I've tried to pass on myself to them.

There has come to light an artefact that, although not related directly to Doris Glanville, has historical links to all the people that have at some time lived in Hele Square. There had been, as far back as any memory goes, a chestnut tree in the centre of the Square. Several people who have given their memories for my first book 'Memories from the Mill' and to this collection, have mentioned the Mill-owning Hepburn family and the tree which some said had a plaque at it denoting that Lady Hepburn had planted the tree in memory of her son, Roger, who had died in the First World War.

Roger Paul Hepburn was a Second Lieutenant in the Royal Engineers, as a Signal Officer to 21st Infantry Brigade. 'Roger Paul Hepburn M C.....aged 24 years, after serving his King and Country for three years in the Great War died of his wounds near Ypres, Belgium on the 3rd August 1917.' He was awarded the Military Cross. (ref: of this in item The Visitors Book, page 86)

Lady Hepburn could have planted the chestnut tree after the war, as the species does grow quickly and to a good size, and photographs of it in my first book, pages 57 and 108, are dated about 1950 and show a very large tree. If one was planted in about 1918 then there must have been an earlier tree that was replaced. Hazel Rowland, again in my first book, described a tree as she remembered it from about 1915 onwards in the centre of Hele Square as a large tree that was pruned to give light to the windows of the houses.

The plaque that has been found states on it

'THIS TREE WAS PLANTED BY ROGER P HEPBURN ON THE FIRST DAY OF THE TWENTIETH CENTURY 1 JANUARY 1901'

It was made of brass with four corner holes in it for attachment to a back plate. The size was 100 by 150 mm. It had been kept in the Mill at Hele and there could be a presumption that it related to Hele rather than to a tree planted in Bradninch, even though the family of Hepburn lived there, at Dunmore House. When Roger planted his tree and the plaque was made he would have been aged eight, so a big event for a small boy. One has to still surmise as to the site of his tree.

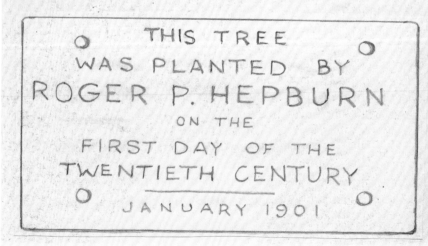

MEN AND MACHINES IN THE LATE 1940'S

Illustration of a Papermaking Machine. From the front, left: Frank Miller, Gordon Pidgeon, Jack Squire, Management Person (in suit). On the right; Jim Vicary.

On the following pages;

1) Turbine house with Ern Thomas
2) Rag Boilers with Freddie Coxhead
3) Wood Pulpier with Bert Bryant
4) Pulp Mixer   this one is untitled and person unidentified
5) Dry End of Papermaking Machine with Gilbert Maddock

Original photographs taken in Hele Mills by E.C.Harris, who was then a professional photographer and owned the Newsagents in the High Street, Bradninch. (Photograph on this page, date unknown).

Followed by   6)   The Rag Room Workers, approx. mid 1940's.Top left, Dick Carpenter, Foreman, centre back, Ena Heard, top right, Jimmy Rew, seated extreme right, Beatie Pollard, (ref. item written by her in first book, page 19).

100

There was a publication called the TRADE MARKS JOURNAL that was published at the Patent Office and printed by The Stationery Office. It came out every week and the one for the Wednesday, 11th May in 1921 was of interest in that it had recorded in it the registration of seven water marks to Hele Mill. That journal was VOL. 46 – No. 2250 and priced at one shilling.

From the letter that was with the journal it seems that the company Wiggins, Teape & Co., (1919) Ltd. had bought the Devon Valley Mill at Hele and was registering the trade marks that had been used there for some time. This would have been good business practice so that no other company could copy and produce the same product lines and claim them for their own. Maybe copyrights had not been a problem in earlier times, but was considered important by 1921 for a company's paper lines. The letter, dated 19th May 1921, was written to the Manager, Mr. John Horsburgh, of the Hele Mill from the main office of Wiggins Teape at 10 & 11 Aldgate in London.

Mr. Horsburgh was well known in Hele and his name occurs several times in items of the history of the Mill. His wife was of the Hepburn family that had owned the mill earlier in the twentieth century.

The seven watermarks were most likely the most important paper lines that were being produced and so were worth protecting. On the following page they are copied here as illustrations as laid out in the journal, but the book is old and the print is not too clear so they are printed in type below.

Watermark B407,982

Primrose

Bank

Watermark B408,241; user claimed from 28th June 1907.

DEVON

EXTRA STRONG

Watermark B408,242; user claimed from 24th May 1892.

ORIGINAL
HELE MILLS
DEVON

Watermark B408, 243; user claimed from 27th September 1904.

DEVON VALLEY
PARCHMENT

Watermark B408,244; user claimed from 24th June 1904.

DEVON VALLEY
SUPERFINE

Watermark B408,245; user claimed from 8th June 1904.

431 MILL
DEVON

Watermark B408,246; user claimed from 28th May 1906.

DEVON VALLEY
LEDGER

Information below the symbols gave details of the Company:-   'Paper except Paperhangings. WIGGINS TEAPE & Co. (1919) LIMITED, 10, Aldgate, London, E.1; and Devon Valley Mill, Hele, near Cullompton, Devonshire; Paper makers Wholesale and Export Stationers. – 29th September, 1920.'

The seven Watermarks as laid out in the Trade Mark Journal of 1921.

Primrose .
Bank

DEVON
EXTRA STRONG

ORIGINAL
HELE MILLS
DEVON

DEVON VALLEY
PARCHMENT

DEVON VALLEY
SUPERFINE

431 MILL
DEVON

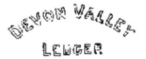

DEVON VALLEY
LEDGER

This extract from 26th May, 1...
No.9 248   Paper, except paperhangings Wiggins, Teape & Co. (1919) Limited, 91, Aldgate,
London, E.1; and Devon Valley Mill, Hele, near Cullompton, Devonshire; Paper Makers and
Wholesale and Export Stationers. 26th September, 1920.

Description on construction of watermark patterns in item 'Watermark of John Dewdney', page 10.
Illustrations of Dandy Stereos, the fine wire designs used to press into the wet paper during
production can be seen in my first book 'Memories from the Mill', item 27, pages 133-4, and also
description of the production skill, item 20, pages 87-88.

A few sheets of headed notepaper that were used by the Paper Mill in the early part of the twentieth century have survived. This gives us a glimpse back to those times. Illustrations of them follow.

Item 1   This is the earliest letter heading as the date is printed as of the nineteenth century. It has beautiful script writing. Called Hele Works, address just Cullompton, Devon. It also simply states that goods and telegrams etc. were to go to Hele Station. That is of interest as it does not include Bradninch in the title so that must have been added later by the railway. Paper watermark JOYNSON 1869.

Item 2.   This headed paper is simple. It gives it as Hele Paper Works and the address, again, just as Cullompton, Devon. Telegrams simply to 'Hepburn Hele' and so it was used during the time the Hepburn family owned the Mill. That would have been up to 1919 in the twentieth century. The delivery of goods was important with the station listed as Hele & Bradninch (GWR). Paper of this and items 3 to 6 watermarked DEVON EXTRA STRONG.

Item 3   Elaborate headed paper in graded shades of blue on cream paper. Used with a date 14th November 1903 typed on it. The Company is now Hele Paper Co. Ltd. but the address is still Hele Paper Works, followed by, Cullompton, Devon, again. The Company title is emphasised with borders and line details. The word Cullompton seems over emphasized, by shading and scrolls but perhaps it was needed for country-wide identification. For the first time information that the Mill was established in 1765. Products listed under the company title, with 'makers of Writing, Drawing, Cartridge & Ledger papers'. Also 'telegraphic address Hepburn Hele', and now 'Goods and Passenger Station – Hele Station G W R 100 yards'.

Item 4   This is a note-let heading of the Hepburn ownership. 1919 is written in pencil on it. This is a simple letter heading but with a more complex script type than item 2 and has the same information except that the address is now Devon Valley Mill instead of Hele Paper Works. Rubber stamped on the top indicated paper production was 'under government control' due no doubt to it being still under First World War conditions.

Item 5   This is the most elaborate sample, shades of blue on cream paper. The date 1919 written in pencil on it, again gives an era for it. It has the Under Government Control printed, not just rubber stamped as on item 4. So this design must have been used a lot during the War years prior to 1919. It is so elaborate it is hard to fully describe. The company title is The Hele Paper Company Ltd. within borders, scrolls, and designed shapes in shades of blue. It takes up nearly all the width of the sheet with 'makers of Writing, Ledger, Drawing, Envelope & Blotting Papers' under the Company title and within the design. Also within the design below this is a primrose logo incorporating the words around it 'Devon Valley Mill'. This logo was used extensively by the Mill in promotions in the twentieth century, not only on letter heading but also as a watermark on special lines of paper, and as a stain glass design in the entrance door to the Mill. Obviously in the early decades a more elaborate image for the company was used due to the awareness of the importance of self-promotion. It seems that the war may have caused changes for industry and communications became more complex. Paper Mills had a government registered number, Hele Mill no was 431 printed at the centre top. The station is now Hele and Bradninch G W R with the telephone now connected to the Mill, listed as Exeter 6. That is a real find for a historian, that 'our' Hele Mill had such an early number; it must have linked up when a telephone exchange first opened in Exeter. It also shows it was an important business and that the management saw early on the value of that new method of communication. Telegrams still came to Hepburn, Hele; but with 'code 5th edition A B C' added to that older simple address. The address was Devon Valley Mill, Hele near Cullompton, Devonshire. For the first time Hele within the address and without emphasis on the word Cullompton. The Mill site had obviously made itself known on the industrial map of the country. On the left were the watermarks of the products: Devon Valley Bond, Devon Valley Ledger, Devon Valley Superfine, Devon Valley Parchment, Devon Extra Strong, Original Hele Mills Devon, Lorna Doone, Devonia and Primrose Bank. At the bottom of the page is printed 'This is our Devon Extra Strong writing and typewriting paper'.

Item 6   This paper heading is very elaborate, on cream paper with complex script with flowing letters. This is of interest as it is just a memorandum sheet, half size of the writing papers. It has 1915-19 written on it in pencil, plus 'under government control' rubber-stamped on the top and so again, if correct, dates it. On the left the company name is written in fine script as The Hele Paper Company Limited. It has the word 'from' just above this with 'memorandum' at the top. In the centre is the primrose symbol as described in item 5. This time it is very prominent, large, and with the plant design in deep yellow on a black background, again with the name of the Mill in a circle around it. It has the number 19 for the century date, and an elaborate 'to' with lines drawn for the receiver's name and address. The address is Devon Valley Mill, Hele, near Cullompton, Devon. The Station, telephone number and telegram details the same as on item 5.

Item 7   The last sample is a very different letter sheet. It has such an elaborate pictorial design to be almost thought of as to represent an art company. It is printed on thick, deep cream, paper. Held up to the light reveals a watermark of one of the Mill products, Devon Extra Strong. The design is elaborate across the top with scrolls and leaves within which is The Hele Paper Co. Ltd. address as Hele Paper Works Near Cullompton Devon; makers of Writing Ledger Drawing Envelope & Blotting papers. Information gives Telegrams: Hepburn Hele and Station: Hele & Bradninch G W R; with no telephone number listed. This means that this sheet could have been earlier, back in the first decade of the century. Products are drawn in a column on the left-hand side, listing - For every sort of commercial stationery, Devon Extra strong, Devon Valley Superfine, Devon Valley Parchment, Mill 431 tubsized, Lorna Doone. Then – For Account books etc, DevonValley Ledger, Original Hele Mills. And then - Blotting, at the bottom.

The quality of these headed papers and the image portrayed by them, plus the complexity and cost of some of these printed papers, shows they must have been of some importance to the management in promoting the business.

Item 1.   Item 2

Hele Works.
Cullompton, Devon.

18

GOODS, TELEGRAMS, &c
TO HELE STATION.

HELE PAPER WORKS.
CULLOMPTON,
DEVON.

TELEGRAMS:-"HEPBURN, HELE"
STATION:- HELE & BRADNINCH, (G.W.R.)

THE HELE PAPER CO LTD

Item 3   Item 4

MILL ESTABLISHED 1765.

HELE PAPER WORKS.

Cullompton, DEVON.

HELE PAPER Co. Ltd.

Makers of
WRITING DRAWING CARTRIDGE
& LEDGER PAPERS.

Telegraphic Address:-"HEPBURN. HELE."

GOODS & PASSENGER STATION—
HELE STATION. G.W.R. 100 YARDS.

HELE PAPER WORKS,
Cullompton, 14th November 1903.
DEVON.

1919

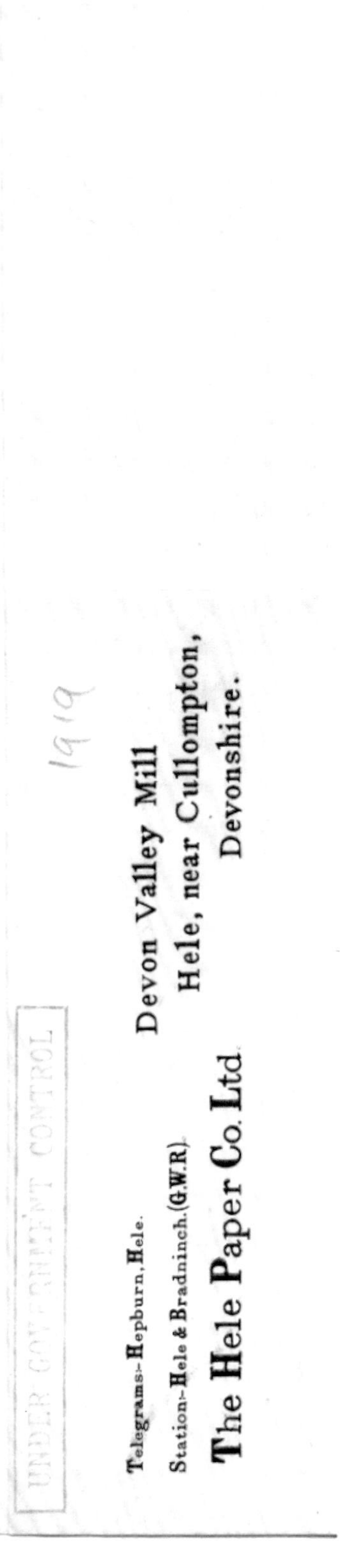

UNDER GOVERNMENT CONTROL

Telegrams:- Hepburn. Hele.

Station:- Hele & Bradninch. (G.W.R)

The Hele Paper Co. Ltd

Devon Valley Mill
Hele, near Cullompton,
Devonshire.

111

Item 5   Item 6

Item 7

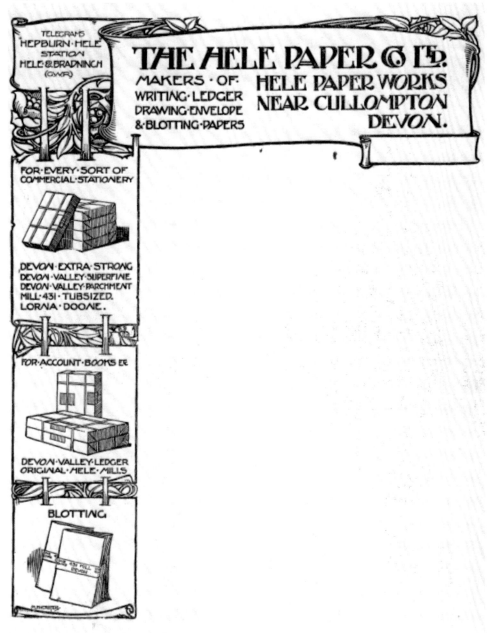

A few examples of the advertisements of paper produced have survived and are illustrated on the following pages. They have been reduced in size and as some details are hard to read, typed copy is adjacent. They indicate the time, especially one or two, which showed the patriotic spirit in the First World War years. Item 1.

Price List.

DEVON VALLEY LEDGER	-	4¾d. per lb.
ORIGINAL HELE MILLS, DEVON		4d. "
DEVON, EXTRA STRONG—		
Large Post, 21lbs. and over	-	5d. per lb.
" " 18 " - -	-	5¼d. "
" " 15 " - -	-	6d. "
DEVON VALLEY PARCHMENT—		
Large Post, 18lbs. and over	-	3½d. per lb.
" " 15 " - -	-	4½d. "
" " 13 " - -	-	5½d. "
" " 11 " - -	-	6d. "
Medium 21 and 23lbs. -	-	3½d. "
" 15lbs. - -	·	5d. "
" 13 " - -	·	5½d. "
Double Foolscap, 30lbs. -	-	3½d. "
" " 20 " -	·	4¼d. "
DEVON VALLEY SUPERFINE		3½d. "
HELE TUB-SIZED VELLUM	-	3½d. "

These papers can be Plate-glazed and Linen-finished at an extra price according to substance and quantity.

MILL 431 TUB-SIZED (BLUE)	-	3¼d. per lb.
E.S. AZURE LAID - -	-	2½d. "
431 MILL BLOTTING -	-	3½d. "
PLAIN BLOTTING - -	-	3¼d. "
MOUNTING BOARDS -	-	4½d. "

Special Prices for Quantities.

Price List. DEVON VALLEY LEDGER – 4¾d. per lb. ORIGINAL HELE MILLS, DEVON 4d : DEVON EXTRA STRONG --- Large post, 21 lbs. and over –5d per lb.:18 -- 5¼d. : 15 -- 6d : DEVON VALLEY PARCHMENT ---Large Post, 18lbs. and over – 3½d. per lb. : 15 -- 4½d. : 13 -- 5½d. : 11 -- 6d. : Medium 21 and 23lbs. – 3½d : 15lbs. – 5d. : 13 -- 5½d. : Double Foolscap, 30lbs. – 3½d. : 20 -- 4¼d. : DEVON VALLEY SUPERFINE 3½d. : HELE TUB-SIZED VELLUM 3½d. These papers can be Plate-glazed and Linen- finished at an extra price according to substance and quantity. MILL 431 TUB-SIZED (BLUE) -- 3¼d. per lb.: E.S. AZURE LAID -- 2½d. : 431 MILL BLOTTING -- 3½d. : PLAIN BLOTTING -- 3¼d. : MOUNTING BOARDS -- 4½d. : Special prices for Quantities.

Item 2.

Made in the West Country.

Stocked in Laid and Wove.

LARGE POST 16½ × 21ins. : : 18, 21, 23lbs.
MEDIUM : 18 × 23ins. : : : 21, 23lbs.
DOUBLE F'CAP. 17 × 27ins. : : 26, 28, 30lbs.
480 Sheets per Ream.

3$^{D.}$ per lb.

Terms : 5% Monthy A/c.

The Hele Paper Co. Ltd.

Hele Mills,

Cullompton, Devonshire.

about 1910

Sample of Wove 21 lbs. Large post LORNA DOONE Made in the West Country. Stocked in Laid and Wove. Large Post 16½ x 21 ins. : : 18, 21, 23 lbs. Medium : 18 x 23 ins. : 21, 23 lbs. Double F'cap. 17 x 27 ins. : 26, 28, 30 lbs. 480 Sheets per Ream. 3 d per lb. Terms : 5% Monthly A/c. The Hele Paper Co. Ltd. Hele Mills, Cullompton, Devonshire.
(This item has 'about 1910' written on it in pencil.)

Item 3.   Featured in The Sales and Wants Advertiser dated March 16, 1914.

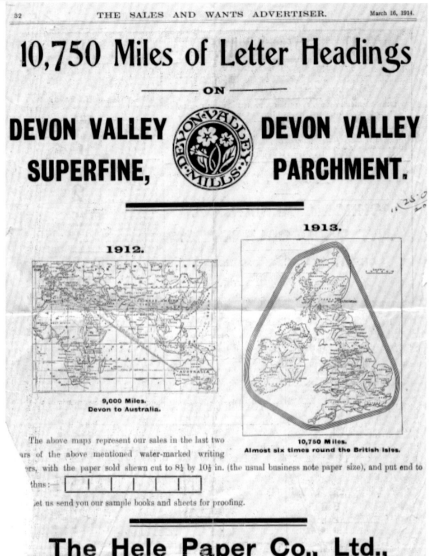

10,750 Miles of Letter Headings on DEVON VALLEY SUPERFINE, DEVON VALLEY PARCHMENT. (between the above words the Primrose symbol with the words Devon Valley Mills around it). (Below are two maps. On the left a map of part of the world with a straight line superimposed on it from Devon to Australia. '1912' above it and '9,000 Miles. Devon to Australia' below it. On the right a map of the British Isles with 5 lines encircling it. With '1913' above it and '10,750 miles. Almost six times round the British Isles.' below it.)

The above maps represent our sales in the last two years of the above mentioned water-marked writing papers, with the paper sold shewn cut to 8¼ by 10½ in. (the usual business note paper size), and put end to end thus:-- Let us send you our sample books and sheets for proofing. The Hele Paper Co., Ltd., Devon Valley Mills, Hele, Nr. Cullompton, Devon. Makers of the best Writing, Typewriting and Ledger Papers, and Papers for the Offset Press.

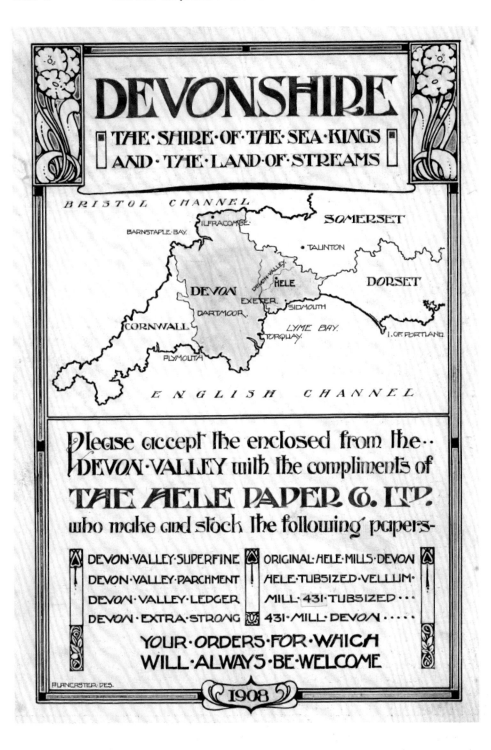

Item 4 (on previous page)
DEVONSHIRE THE SHIRE OF THE SEA KINGS AND THE LAND OF STREAMS
(map of the West Country showing Devon coloured pink, the counties and some towns, the Bristol
and English Channels identified, and Hele and Devon Valley marked above Exeter.)
Please accept the enclosed from the Devon.Valley mill with complements of THE HELE PAPER
CO. LTD. who make and stock the following papers – Devon Valley Superfine; Original Hele Mills
Devon; Devon Valley Parchment; Hele Tubsized Vellum; Devon Valley Ledger; Mill 431 Tubsized;
Devon Extra Strong; 431 Mill Devon. Your order for which will always be welcome. 1908

Item 5.   printed on Devon Valley 431 Mill watermarked Blotting paper.

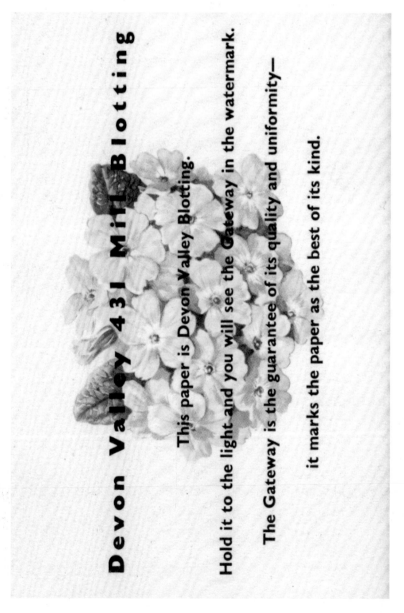

Devon Valley 431 Mill Blotting. This paper is Devon Valley Blotting. Hold it to the light and you
will see the Gateway in the watermark. The Gateway is the guarantee of its quality and uniformity – it
marks the paper as the best of its kind.

118

Item 6.   Hand drawn sketch of an advertisement design for the Hele Paper Company Ltd.
It is an early example as it ensured that only rags were to be used for that paper. It could
have been the idea of the Management in the Mill but it is not known who drew it or if it
was completed and used.

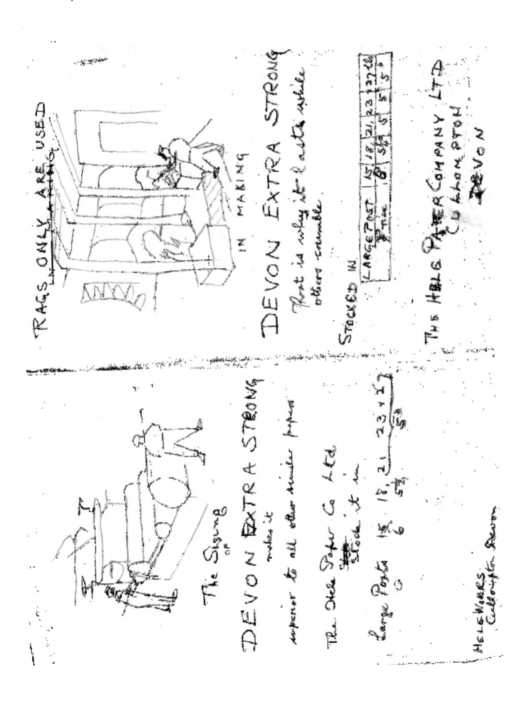

PROMOTIONAL PRIMROSES FROM HELE MILL – Recipients' responses.

Newspaper clippings from 1915 about the promotion of Hele Mills in sending out bunches of primroses in the spring to their customers. The practice must have been going for some years prior to 1915 as some of the recipients remark on having received the gift in previous years. 1915 is significant however, being the early part of the First World War. Maybe it was thought to continue it as a morale booster in a time of national crisis.

A bunch of freshly gathered primroses reached "The Daily Chronicle" office yesterday from the Hele paper Co., of Hele, Devonshire. Every year the firm send this novel form of greeting to their many friends. With the flowers was the message; "In these days of anxiety and trouble our primroses will, we trust, be as welcome as in times of peace. They will perhaps remind you that winter does not last for ever, and help you to see the light of summer days ahead."

from Daily Chronicle. 10-3-15.

Business life is not roses all the way just now, but I have just had experience of a method by which it can be made considerably brighter. ~~ Yesterday when I was just in the throe of a rare struggle against time – in the thick of a press day rush, in fact – I had delivered to me a box from a firm with whom the "Reporter" had business dealings. ~~ The opening of that box gave me the daintiest and most agreeable surprise I have had for a long time. ~~ Instead of finding – as I firmly expected would be the case – some everyday samples, I found three bunches of gorgeous primroses, into which I buried my editorial nose for so long that I felt for the time lifted straight from a work-a-day newspaper office right into the heart of my native Kent. ~~ Accompanying those beautiful flowers was the most cheery of notes, which read thus: "I dreamed that as I wandered by the way, Bare Winter suddenly changed to spring. In these days of anxiety and trouble our primroses will, we trust, be as welcome as in times of peace." ~~ I am not ashamed to confess that I felt all the better for that kindly back-up, and the sweet and dainty flowers that accompanied it. ~~ And in order that all the world may know the authors of my good fortune, let me say it was from the Hele Paper Co., whose works are in "Devon, glorious Devon."

from St Helens Reporter.

We are again indebted to the Hele Paper Co. Ltd., of Devon Valley Mill, Hele, Cullompton, Devonshire, for a graceful and charming reminder that Bare Winter has suddenly changed to Spring. As usual it takes the form of a box of primroses, and one scarcely knows which to admire most - the beautiful flower itself, or the kindly courtesy which inspires the gift. Redolent with the

120

fragrance of Devon's beautiful valleys, it is also expressive of a benevolent consideration for those who toil and live in less favoured regions, which is all too rare. The Hele Paper Company, further, sent to the recipients of their delightful offering the following gracious message, which we have no doubt found a grateful response in many publishing and printing offices in this country: "In these days of anxiety and trouble, our primroses will, we trust, be as welcome as in times of peace. They will perhaps remind you that winter does not last for ever, and help you to see the light of sunnier days ahead."

from The Paper Maker. 1-4-15.

BUSINESS COURTESIES. It would seem difficult to associate the primrose - that beautiful harbinger of Spring - with business. And yet during the early days of March in each year there comes to many a printing office a dainty box of these earliest flowers from the Devon valley. ... Culled from the sheltered vales of Devon, backed by their own exquisitely veined foliage, came on Tuesday a box of primroses, in little posies. "Bare Winter suddenly was changed to Spring." Everything was in perfect taste. It needs a genius to send a message with a posy to a business house, no less than it needs an artist to bunch the modest primrose. So one appreciated the gracious message that accompanied the gift. It was as follows: "In these days of anxiety and trouble, our Primroses will, we trust, be as welcome as in times of peace. They will perhaps remind you that winter does not last for ever, and help you to see the light of sunnier days ahead."
The thoughts which the primroses inspire could not have been more aptly expressed, and the Hele Paper Company have rendered a distinct service in sending the fragile primroses as a reminder of the beautiful things that lie hidden in almost un-dreamt-of places. The primrose will bloom in the shelter of a huge boulder and amid stern and almost forbidding surroundings. In a charming reference to "Spring on the Dorset Coast," a correspondent says: "At Axminster one afternoon I saw a khaki-clad soldier at the railway station carrying a bunch of wild daffodils." Spring flowers are never out of place, and this is why a commercial firm can express a delightful business courtesy in a bunch of primroses.   from Smethwick telephone. 13-3-15.

The Hele Paper Company sends from Cullompton a box of primroses to remind the Cardiff receivers that "Winter does not last for ever," and to "help them see the light of sunnier days ahead." But the Hele Paper Company must not be proud; Cardiff has had primroses since Christmas, and will not take a back seat to Cullompton or anywhere else. All the same, it is a kindly greeting on Cullompton's part.   from South Wales Daily News. 10-3-15.

Following page; Letter in Gateway Magazine No. 68, Wiggins Teape Group, September 1977. Primrose Design by Sophie Nash, aged 14. 2004.
Memories of sending of the primroses in my first book 'Memories from the Mill': item page 61.

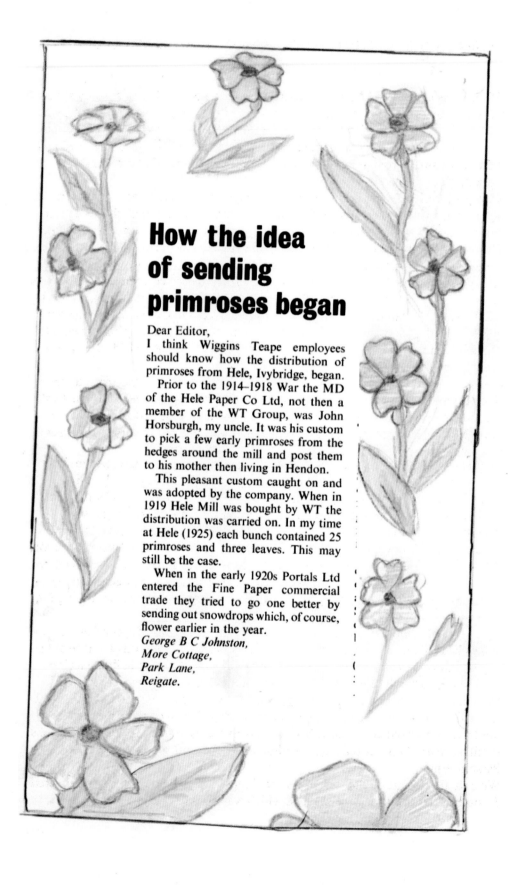

How the idea of sending primroses began

Dear Editor,
I think Wiggins Teape employees should know how the distribution of primroses from Hele, Ivybridge, began.

Prior to the 1914–1918 War the MD of the Hele Paper Co Ltd, not then a member of the WT Group, was John Horsburgh, my uncle. It was his custom to pick a few early primroses from the hedges around the mill and post them to his mother then living in Hendon.

This pleasant custom caught on and was adopted by the company. When in 1919 Hele Mill was bought by WT the distribution was carried on. In my time at Hele (1925) each bunch contained 25 primroses and three leaves. This may still be the case.

When in the early 1920s Portals Ltd entered the Fine Paper commercial trade they tried to go one better by sending out snowdrops which, of course, flower earlier in the year.

George B C Johnston,
More Cottage,
Park Lane,
Reigate.

CYDERMAKING AT WHITEWAYS – MEMORIES OF JUNE BOLT.

When I was at school I had a great wish to become a Nurse, but after study at East Devon College I was disappointed in that possibility. I decided to go to the Cyder Factory of Whiteways in Hele. It felt a familiar place to start out on my working life as my father and grandfather had worked there before me. I went in 1976 and there was a small group of about nine or twelve friendly people there on the working floor.

Workers for the Whiteway family and the Management were treated as valued people and so stayed for most of their working lives; not only that, the hours were fair and the pay was very high for the area. I got £42 a week when I first started. This was good even though better money was made in the nearby Paper Mill; but there you had to work the shift system with one shift going through the night and also working through the weekend. We finished at 5 o'clock each day and later as the hours were reduced through national agreements we ended the week at mid-day on Fridays. My family often went off for the weekend to Cornwall, leaving our home in Bradninch early Saturday morning, travelling by ordinary bus services to Plymouth, to be there mid-morning to be picked up by a relative and so on to the country and sea.

On my first day I walked into the works at Hele and said 'good-morning' to the first person I met. It was an older gentleman and he looked at me and replied with the same words, then asked my name. I told him I was June and he said he had never had anyone named that working for him so I would be the first. The other girls told me he was Mr. Whiteway himself, but as I was polite so was he.

To go back to earlier days, ones I obviously didn't know personally, just to show you the personal caring nature of the members of the Whiteway family. My grandfather was Charles James (Jim) Rew and he was working as a Cooper with the large wooden barrels they used then. The barrels were six feet high when upended and he was on top of them and slipped and fell down between two. He badly injured all down his spine and had to be taken to hospital in Exeter. The Mr. Whiteway of that time organised all the arrangements and even got a waterbed for the extra comfort of my granddad while there. He was in for six weeks and my grandmother could go in to visit him several times with Mr. Whiteway paying for the taxi fare.

By the time I went to work at Whiteways in Hele the making of cyder from local apples had already stopped, about eight years previously. That was all done at the bigger main depot at Whimple. At Hele we worked in the main building and us girls filled the two litre jars and five gallon poly barrels. They were gravity fed from the large vats in the room above. The jars or barrels were full when the float reached the top. The apples in the orchards were picked and taken to Shepton Mallet to be pressed and it came back in tankers for us to fill. We had other drinks to fill, such as Sherry as pale dry, medium dry and cream, Damson Mead and Parsnip Wine.

We only filled large containers, never into bottles, and the products were delivered To outlets to be bottled on or to pubs, which wanted it as draught. It was the practice that we worked as a team and we could in general do all the different tasks so that if anyone was away ill we could fill in and the work was not held up. Of course the men did the heavier work and some of it was especially so although there was a forklift truck to use for the heaviest lifting. When the works finally closed in Hele I worked over in Whimple for about four years before it all closed down.

To get an idea of what it was like before my time there, my mother is a mine of information because the family worked there back for three generations. On her side the family can be traced back to living at Worth Cottages in Hele. Great-granddad William Rew lived there and my mother remembers all the family. His brother George and his family lived in the other one of the pair of cottages and both worked for Mr. Wellington of Worth Farm. The eldest son of Great-granddad, John, stayed local and was living next to his father in Great-uncle George's cottage in 1901. The third son, Uncle Tom, was born in 1887 and he went to work in the Rhondda Valley in Wales when he was fourteen and became a Hustler, that is he took care of the ponies underground in the coalmines.

Charles, the next son, was born three years later and he was my grandfather. He also went to work in the coalmines with his brother but he came back to Devon in 1926. He worked in the Paper Mill in Hele. At the outbreak of war in 1939 he was put on war work. This resulted in him having to leave the Mill and he had to work for Whiteways to make cyder. This may have seemed a strange idea but when you think about it the country needed all the food and drink it could produce for itself as it was very difficult to import products from abroad.

My grandparents lived at Moorland Cottage in Hele, and my mother says she liked growing up and living at Moorland, it had a lovely view. At Moorland Cottage they could easily walk over the field by a footpath and on down Hilly Lane into the centre of Hele village and Square. There were three fields along Hilly Lane then but only one large one now.

The workers were so friendly together out of work as well as in it. They had many good laughs and many activities spent together in Bradninch. There used to be a special trick within work of leaving a rotten apple on a chair and everyone at sometime got caught by it by sitting on it. Outside of work there was a well remembered trick of putting a brick or sometimes two into the saddlebag of a friend and complaining on the way home that he was slow cycling that day and maybe he had a flat tyre making him work so hard at cycling up to Bradninch. That always made the friend stop and realise he had been caught once more.

My grandfather was a very busy, practical man and the others usually came to the cottage on a Sunday morning to chat and often to get their bikes seen to by him. My grandfather was also good at the garden and liked working outside. Moorland Cottage is no longer there, it was pulled down and a new house was built in the grounds.

My mother was christened Ellen after her mother as I am also. She however was given a second Christian name of Amy and has always been known by that; even today although her married name is Bolt, some of her older acquaintances still call her Amy Rew; and even call me June Rew but I say to them I am also half June Bolt. It is just that the Rew family have lived in and around Bradninch for so many generations and my father, Percy Bolt, came into the parish coming from Broadclyst, so it is said as a kind of local joke calling him an incomer. My father started out in life as a market gardener working for his parents who had a market garden business in Broadclyst. When he came to Whiteways he became the Cellar Man. He and my mother married in 1955 and they lived at Broadclyst. Sadly their first child, my sister, died very young but I came along in 1958.

My uncle Jim, Jim Rew, brother to my mother, has worked all his life at the Paper Mill in Hele where he started as Lodge Boy under Mr. Wallends, the Lodge-Keeper.

Going back to cydermaking in my father's and grandfather's times it was very much a local activity using the apples in the orchards alongside and supplemented by all the local farmers bringing apples by the cartloads. In the height of the apple-picking season they were queuing along the road leading to the works as each wagon was weighed as it was delivered.

There were many different important jobs with the apple-pressing. There was the Cooper such as my granddad, to make, repair and keep the wooden barrels in good order. There was the pressing to see to and after that the fermenting of the apple juice and the storing in the large vats.

It was especially busy in the Autumn with work going on until nine o'clock in the evening and again with the bottling up before Christmas. The workers were given a Christmas bonus and also a choice of two bottles of any item produced. The favourite choices were Glendewi and Sherry. Keeping in with the seasons there was another benefit at Easter – two bottles of cyder on top of pay for working on Good Friday. It was a tradition to do gardening on that day in the orchards. The apple trees were of course cared for all year round with apple-picking the busiest time with extra workers in, and then in the New Year with the pruning of the trees.

Family history of the family of Rew.
There are Census records of the family of Rew living in both Worth Cottages on Worth Farm in Hele. Some details of the censuses for Worth Cottages are in this book, page 36.

A SHORT HISTORY OF CYDER-MAKING IN HELE.

Prior to 1934 there were several orchards of apple species that were very suitable for the production of cyder. They were laid out around the area of the old A38 main road at Hele Cross. This was on the opposite side of the river from the Paper Mill. The railway ran along close by. The orchards were on the rising ground on the north facing side of the valley and so were above the river flood plain.

In 1934 the Cyder Works had been owned by a renowned company, Schweppes Ltd and run from an office in Bristol. It was described as 'A small cyder factory at Hele between railway and the A 38 main road with twenty-five acres of excellent orchards.'

The area encompassed land under Spatland owned by Thomas Martin and Bindles already identified as orchards on the Tythe map of 1841. There followed the building of a large house on Spatland field, which became Hillside House, that

stands now right on the junction of the roads at Hele Cross. It was a fine stone-built substantial house maybe by its style linked to the building of the Station and Hotel at Hele with the arrival of the Railway; or alternatively and most probably built for a member of the Aclands, the local landed gentry of Killerton. Members of that family certainly lived there later as in the mid-twentieth century a Lady Acland told how when she was a child she visited an Aunt who lived there. She remembered the wonderful grapes in the greenhouse and mulberries from a tree in the garden. Hillside House had fine gardens, coach-house, tennis court and gardener's cottage. That last is a separate dwelling today known as Lower Hillside. The main house owned the private water supply in a higher orchard and the sewerage system in the lower orchard of the later Cyder Works, as well as retaining control over certain conditions on the later Cyder Works. That indicates that Hillside House was involved with the setting up of cyder-making at Hele.
In the West Country soil and climate suited apple trees and so cyder was a basic farm workers drink. There developed many varieties of apples, most of very local spread, and it can be assumed that in the orchards in Hele there were examples of the older local apples. The farming family of Whiteway from Totnes, in Devon, became known as good cyder-makers and Henry, the founder of the Whiteway Cyder firm, was born there in 1853. The family moved to Whimple in East Devon in 1878 and in 1897 a company was formed, Henry Whiteway and Co. It became a public company in 1934, Whiteways Cyder Co. Ltd. and in that same year purchased the Hele factory and orchards of Schweppes Ltd. and so Hele cyder-making became part of the large local company. Schweppes's Hele holding was bought for £16,310, made up partly of hydraulic apple presses, oak vats for 300,000 gallons, a good artesian well, a steam engine with dynamo weighbridge, drying equipment, land and buildings at £6,000, with the Manager's house valued at £210. It had supplied the local firm of brewers, Starkey Knight & Ford. Schweppes employed nine men with Mr. A. Robins as the manager. Whiteways kept all the employees on and the firm continued to expand and in 1972 became Whiteways of Whimple Ltd. However its commercial success declined and in June 1986 it was merged into Vine Products Ltd. and finally production ceased in Whimple all together and also of course in Hele as that works was part of the same company. The factory works were sold and the orchards around it went to different buyers. Some, mainly the ones on the higher side of the main A38 road, were uprooted and the land reverted to pasture. The ones close in to the works remained as old orchards and have been maintained and cropped up to this present day.

The illustration on the following page is of an early twentieth century deed map of the area. Followed by an illustration of a photograph from the early 1950's of some of the employees of Whiteways Cyder Factory.
Identifying from the left in the front: Mr. Brooks; Edgar Burnell (behind); Mr. Bryant;
     from the right in the front: Archie Robins; Mr. Radford (behind); Les Turner;
         'Jim' Charlie Rew, Grandfather (right at the back); Mr. Newman.

Reference for the history of Whiteways is 'Whiteways Cyder – a company history' by E.V.M. Whiteway 1990.
Separate items in this book, Olden Hele, page 172, and Bindles Orchard, page183, refer to this area.

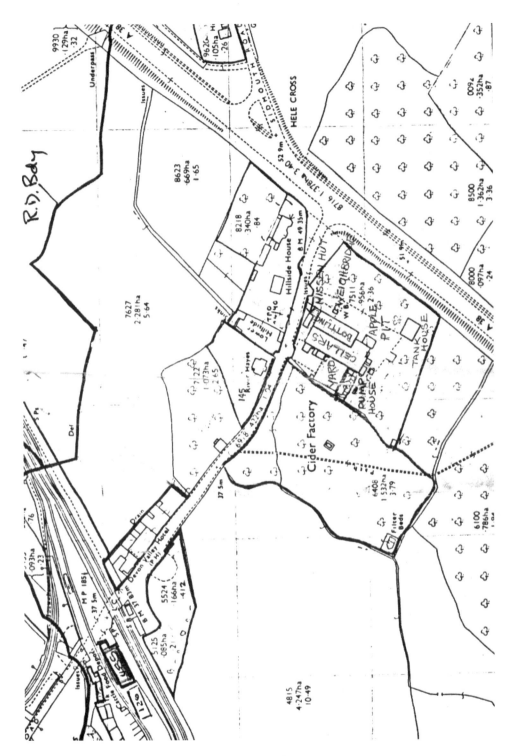

Illustration from an early twentieth century Deed Map. The areas in the Cyder Factory
marked – Cellars, Bottling, Tank House, Pump House, Weighbridge, Apple Pit, Yard.
Further information has been found on the history of the apple orchards in Hele in the separate item
on Bindle's Orchards, page 183.

127

CYDERMAKING AT WHITEWAYS -- MEMORIES OF EDGAR BURNELL.

I have spent nearly the whole of my working life at Whiteways Cyder Works at Hele. I can list all the different jobs I have done there and will do so later. I turned my hand to all the different skills and activities involved in running the 'Factory', which is what we often called the works. I started as an ordinary labourer and ended as Works-Foreman at the end. In-between I had been shovelman, pressman, rackman, cellarman, cooper, engineer and mechanic, stand-in Manager for six months and with the side role of company first-aider. Name any other task and I will add it to the list.

I suppose I had a feeling for cyder making because my father had been employed as the cyder man to the Squire of Clyst Hydon, Mr.Huysh. He produced cyder for him on his land there. In fact there were apple trees in plenty in this east area of Devon, going through into Dorset and Somerset so it was made on many farms.

I went straight into the R.A.F. when I grew up because the Second World War was on and I guess it was about in 1947, after two years there, I came out and started in Hele for the Whiteways firm. I started as a labourer and the wages were slightly higher than the ordinary agricultural wages on the farms around. I was quite handy with mechanical skills so I was soon involved in the machinery that was so important in the factory. By the time I was in charge of the maintenance of them I knew all the processes of producing apple juice, and later as the firm improved its process and expanded I often taxed my brain to work the innovations to the system. For example at a later time, after the cyder making finished at Hele in about 1967 although it continued at Whimple, our factory changed to become a bottling-up plant. This meant that products were brought to us in liquid bulk which we stored, and then filled casks and poly containers, which were then sent to customers.

We had to remove much of the existing pumping fixtures and equipment. Then we had to somehow put the new large container tanks high in the building so that the liquid could be gravity fed down to the main room where the girls filled the smaller containers. It was decided the tanks would have to go into the roof space, and a lot of discussion went on as it was a difficult problem because it seemed we would have not only to dismantle a large part of the structure, of floors and timbers in the centre of the factory, but also to build a strong base for the tanks to sit on once we had got them up there. There were many thoughts with a few wild joke ideas, one being to take the roof off the building, but it gave me a possibility so I said …'why not take out a hole in the side of the roof, removing tiles and timbers; then having already reinforced the loft floor, lift the tanks in with a crane and then replace the roof timbers and tiles.' In fact that is what happened.

Going back to earlier times I can explain the process of cyder making. Most of the year there were about nine of us in the workforce, but this expanded to as many as fifty during the busy Autumn time with casual labourers. The apples had to be picked, there was no distinction between the different types, all went into the Pound House. This was on the side of the building as trucks, handcarts or tractors could tip them in. Local farmers brought in their crop so a weigh-bridge was constructed in the drive to calculate each load for tonnage. There was a small brick building for the equipment and the weighbridge clerk who was usually an employee of the firm from Whimple. Of course if a load was found to have too many rotten apples within it then a sum was deducted. Rotten apples could go in but they didn't have the juice quantity of good apples.

It had been that in some season we even had apples shipped from abroad. They came from Ireland, and they were always all green, no red apples, but they were good. Once we had them from France, but never again. We didn't know what was going wrong but the cutting knives all chipped and broke. I had a fine time mending them and there were sharp noises during the chopping. We then found lots of small pieces of chipping stones that are laid on the railways. We had to give up on that lot of apples. We think the apples had been collected onto the railway lines and in the shovelling into the trucks many small chips of stone went in as well. That was a dead loss to us in apples and in weight.

The apples were put in the apple-pit and chopped by long knives on a circular mill, and these I would maintain, set and sharpen. The chopped apples were then put in buckets on an escalator and tipped down into the square wooden boxes which tapered to an outlet above the 'Cheeses'. All the pipes and fittings were of brass or copper; steel pipes would have rusted and contaminated the apple juice.

The Cheeses were constructed with a wooden tray at the base, then a layer of crushed apples was spread over it, then a heavy cloth, rather like blanket or felt material went next with the wooden rack on top. It was built up in those layers and each Cheese usually ended up with about ten racks. Later the cloth was made of man-made material. It took three men to put the folded cloth on top and open it out flat ready for the next spread of apples. The completed Cheese was then moved over to one of four Presses. The whole thing was pressed down to squeeze the juice down and through pipes down to the Cellar. In there the liquid was stored in tanks or vats, which was the lower building to the north of the main working building. We produced pure apple juice at Hele and then let it ferment into alcoholic cyder. There are many theories as to what to add to aid fermentation but we never followed that. Many farmers added a joint of raw meat 'for the apples to work on' and of course there was the myth that adding a dead rat aided the production of good cyder.

The storage tanks were large, made of concrete. Each could hold 25,000 gallons which was about 100 tons of apples. The earlier ones, I remember, were lined with six inch glass tiles and they held 25,000 gallons. There was another tank that had been built up by the hedge to the main road and the liquid apple-juice was pumped up to it. Later they were replaced and the new tanks were lined with a material called Ebon. It was black and came in slabs that were fitted to the inside. The slabs were heated to join together and then it was polished to a shiny surface. Those new tanks were constructed in a new separate building called the Tank House.

The Tank House was a tall separate building to the south of the main Factory buildings. It was very well built of brick with the cyder tanks inside with a pumping system to and from it, to the main building. What is special about it is that it was built by a gang of Italians. This was not long after the Second World

130

War and they came over and completed everything to do with it, structure and plumbing. They all stayed locally with some staying on site in a war-time Nissen hut in the grounds. I think after it was done they moved on to a new job, rather like the travelling craftsmen of old.

Our water came from a reservoir built into the ground in the main orchard on the other side of the main road. This was higher ground and of course the orchard land belonged to the Factory. The water was used for cleaning out all the equipment and the vats etc. We also supplied with water the pub, then called The Railway Inn, which was down the road next to the Railway Station. A pipe was laid down to it from us.

To get back to the cyder process. The apple liquid was pumped into the individual barrels. Those barrels were large, some six foot high, but when full they were stored outside in front of the building on their sides in rows. There were long wooden wedges to keep them in place and more were put on top of the bottom row, even to three tiers. The fermenting cyder was regularly checked. If there was any leak from the joints of the wooden planks of the barrels or at the ends, in fact anywhere where the wood was not tight enough I then became the Caulker Man. This consisted of forcing brown paper into the crack with a special sharp tool known as a caulking tool. Then when the leak was sealed we had to tighten the iron bands around that barrel.

If the cyder was wanted at Whimple or to any other outlet in that large size barrel they could be rolled out of the pile and rolled onto a lorry. It was all done by manpower in those days. Each barrel contained 57 gallons and they would roll eight onto the lorry. Otherwise they went back into the works when ready, to be moved into smaller handy barrels or to be bottled up. Later of course, progress meant a change to the use of tankers to move liquid in bulk, and this again meant more organisation and pipes and pumping systems to load and unload the liquid.

So after an enjoyable working life I retired after thirty-five years in 1979. The family members of the Whiteway family were entirely involved in the company and were careful and successful in business. Even so they were in general good to work for and knew all the workers well. I attended a function to celebrate twenty-five years of service. There is a photograph of it and there must have been about twenty employees from the various works, and we could choose presents valued at fifty pounds. I chose a refrigerator and an electric drill.

Times have changed since I have retired. The works, having closed down, the buildings now belong to an Antiques firm. I went up there once when my son was visiting me and most of the buildings from the outside looked the same. I did discover one item that I personally made that has well and truly lasted. Into the area that had been the Apple Pound I had built into the wall two steps to go down. These had been set deep, of oak, and edged with iron. They were there complete and still in use.

The illustrations on the following page are;
top – March 1972; from the left, Eric Whiteway, Edgar Burnell, Mr. Tucker (Hele Manager), Reg Whiteway (Chairman).
below – Group photo of presentation of 25 years long service awards, to 43 employees.

A SIGNALMAN AT HELE – MEMORIES OF KEN BY CAROL SNELL.

Husband Ken was on the Railway all his working life, mainly as the Relief Signalman for the Exeter area. He only had two years away to do his National Service when he was eighteen. His relief work took him as far as Yeovil on the London line to Barnstable in North Devon. When he was relief at Hele he was on home ground; he could walk or bicycle from home as he lived at Westfield in Bradninch. He looked after his mother and then after we were married we lived in Westfield. Quite a local romance as I had always lived in the same road, just twelve houses downhill, and I had looked after my mother for some years.

Before British Rail automated the signalling system there was twenty-four hour cover at the Hele and Bradninch Box with three men each on eight-hour shifts. Automation meant that the Hele stretch was then covered long distance from further north and south along the line.

The Hele signalman had to work the large gates that were across the rail lines to close the road for trains but after automation they were changed to single bars coming down triggered by the approaching train. There was no personal supervision any more. In fact there was no signal box any more as it was demolished so that all that there now is at Hele is the foundation square alongside the crossing. The station was closed earlier in the 1960's with the waiting room on one side left as the store and rest room for the track maintenance crew.

It used to be such a busy place in Ken's early years at the station with Station Master and Porter and people going to catch trains all day and evenings. Also the goods trains passing through. Even after the station closed people still felt the crossing was a friendly place; the window of the box nearly always open as there was always someone to call out hello to, or a wave up to the signalman in the box. For others there was a drop in to talk to Ken or who ever was on duty and even a pot of tea on the go for the regulars such as George Cornish, the local postman. Those on the further end of the round just had to wait a little longer for their letters. There were sometimes long lines of cars, buses, bikes and tractors etc, maybe sheep and cows occasionally, waiting for the trains, especially the slow 'goods' to go through. A different interference with life at Hele Crossing, when the trains were held up as well, was when the floods arose at Hele. The very highest ones flooded the level crossing and the railway lines.

Ken retired after 47 years on the Railway spending the last years at the new main box at St.Davids Exeter but was not so keen on its air-conditioning, he preferred the open windows. Ken was the signalman who closed the old Exeter West Box when it all changed to the new automation system, which was worked from the New Box. He pulled the last lever. That Box was bought by an enthusiasts group called Exeter West Group. They dismantled it and moved it to the Railway Museum at Crewe. They got a lot of information and advise from Ken and other employees who had worked the box and when it had been reassembled Ken, with Eddie Guerin, another retired Exeter West Box Signalman, was given the honour of 'opening and starting it' in May 1993 up at the Crewe Museum.

[information from the then paper-boy, John Nash, that George Cornish helped him out with the Box delivery if he was late; and occasionally the reverse happened..]   133

Above: Ken Snell 'Relaxing with a cup of tea' in Exeter West Box at Crewe Museum.
ref: Exeter West Group. Below: Hele Station, Signal Box seen beyond waiting area. (from
a postcard) Next page: Hele Crossing and Signal Box. approx. 1970s.
Illustration of railway and Hele flooded on pages 149-150.

135

WELLS – DRAINS – FLOODS – AT HELE MILLS.

FIRST – THE SEARCH FOR WELLS. The Paper Mill over all its working existence had realised the value of the use of the right quality of water to produce high quality paper. It had from time to time explored the area for deep level water and in some cases it found 'gold' in the local hills in the form of pure, plentiful underground springs and water-courses.

We have an early report, an agreement to sink a bore-hole, and two explorations for underground water courses. A report by J.M.Martin of Bradninch Place, Exeter, dated 31st Oct: 1889 to James Hall Esq. was evidence of the interest. It was not written for the Hele Mills but a copy was with the other paperwork on water divining of 1927, so it obviously had been studied and considered relevant. It refers to the Bridge Mill [later called Silverton Mill] which was two miles down river from Hele. 'The Hansard Mills – Increase of Pure Water.'

'I beg to submit the following report on the subject, and to send you herewith a geological section running north and south through your mills and the well on the south side thereof.

The section commences at the road from Exeter to Clyst Honiton and runs to the Clyst Valley; it passes Crabtree, [at junction to Killerton] the Hansard Mills [Bridge Mills] ... and over Copy Down [north of Silverton and Hele Mills] to the neighbourhood of Butterleigh. It exhibits conditions favourable to the acquisition of a large quantity of water at a moderate cost.

...the core of the ridge running from Bradninch to Christ Cross [north of Silverton] in which Copy Down occupies a central position, is composed of carboniferous shale, which is almost impervious to water;... rain on the pervious new Red Sandstone beds which cap the hill and cover its southern slope, being unable to penetrate the shale, follow the planes of stratification... which here dip towards the south........it so happens that in this instance the new Red strata are intercepted and cut across by dykes of trap rock running for the most part almost due east and west. The rock...is of the same character as the large mass which occupies nearly the whole of Killerton Park (once a centre of eruption) and are probably in subterranean connected with it. All this rock is much fissured...it will yield a far larger quantity of water...owing to the greater facility the fissures afford for its passage........The section shows an east and west dyke of trap at the south foot of Copy Down, which if extended eastward would admit the assumption that the Hele well has penetrated it, and account for its productiveness.

Trew's Weir [on the Exe river at Exeter] well also probably penetrates an underground ramification from the volcanic boss of Rougemont. [in Exeter] On no other ground can I account for the large amount of water yielded by it,.....'

J.M.Martin concluded his report with details of well boring and construction and costs. What the management at Silverton Mill did following the information was a different issue to the needs and thoughts of the Hele Mill management and how they used that information.

A different report was also with those papers in Hele Mill. It records two Wells. It had been copied from The British Association for the Advancement of Science for 1879. Those Wells must have been outstanding in their quantity and quality to have been thus registered nationally.

'Particulars of Well at Hele Paper Mills, Hele.

1. Position of Well – Hele Paper Mills.   2. Approximate height of same above mean sea level – 90 ft.   3. Depth of Well – 20ft.   4. Diameter of Well – 10ft. 5. Depth of borehole from surface – 120ft. 6. ins.   6. Diameter of borehole – 6 ins.   7. Water levels – no record as pumps always at work, Sundays excepted. Suction pipes 30ft. below surface.   8. Quantity pumped per day – 295,000 gallons. Water very pure.   9. Nature of formation passed through – New Red Sandstone.

Particulars of Well at Kensham Mills, Hele.

1. Position of Well – Kensham Mills, Hele.   2. Height above mean sea level – about 100ft.   3. Depth dug well below surface – 40ft.   4. Diameter of dug well – 5ft.   Depth of borehole below surface – 200ft.   6. Diameter of borehole – 7ins.   7. Water level – less than30ft. below surface.   8. Quantity of water pumped per day – 170,000 gallons.   9. Borehole pierces the New Red Sandstone.'

Going forward to 1915 we see consideration by the Mill management to find the 'right' spot to sink a new borehole for an extra well. A handwritten reply from Thomas Owen & Co. Ltd of the Ely Paper Works in Cardiff. Dated 25 Feby 1915 to a friendly enquiry from John Horsburgh, the Mananging Director of Hele Mills. 'Dear Sirs, Replying to yours of the 23rd. We have one Artesian Well (about 250 feet) bored by C. Isler & Co which is quite successful. Our last trial was a failure. Isler went down 400 feet & failed to find the water & we gave it up as a bad job. As you suggest there is a good deal of speculation in a job of this sort.   Yours truly   T. Armstead ' [signed]

On the 25th February 1915 the Hele Paper Co. received an estimate from the Isler Company for the proposed sinking of a borehole at Hele. From the headed paper it can be seen they were a well-established firm in this area of work.

'For fixing an $11\frac{1}{2}$ inch diameter Artesian Bored Tube Well, from the surface, into the New Red Sandstone formation, including all labour and use of necessary well boring plant:- 1st 100 feet @ 15s per foot - £75; 2nd 100 feet @ 17s per foot - £85; 3rd 100 feet @ 19s per foot – £95; 4th 100 feet @ 21s per foot – say about 50 feet of $11\frac{1}{2}$ inch diameter C.Isler & Co's special well lining tubes, @16s per foot- £40; One steel shoe for ditto- £5; Fixing plant, - £10. Testing supply on completion, including 48 hours continuous pumping, with plant capable of raising 15,000 gallons per hour if this supply exists, on a lift not exceeding 80 to 100 feet - £35. This totalled £345. If any further pumping required after the above our charge would be at the rate of 45s per day of 9 hours. Steam to be provided by you free of charge, also water for our drill, we to supply the necessary pump for pumping the water. We to sink the necessary pit for the convenience of boring, you to supply the timber for lining same. Carriage and cartage of plant to and fro and men's third class railway fare there and back, extra.

Revised terms of payment:- Cash every fourteen days for work actually completed during that period. 90% of the value of all machinery to be paid on delivery, balance on completion.'

Moving on a decade we find the Mill management still looking for good supplies of underground water. They are now using water divining as a serious and reliable method. The first of two very different reports was from J. Mullins & Sons. Water finders by the Divining Rod Engineers, Railway Place, Bath.

'5th November 1927......Our Mr. H.W.Mullins made an extensive survey, covering all the land owned by your Company, and found that water existed more or less over the whole area. But the lower lands, vis: those that are liable to flood, we should rule out as being unsuitable, and by no means the best situation for obtaining an additional supply......Site No. 1 .... is at the end of the new stores. Here water could be obtained to the extent of about 100,000 gallons a day, the total depth being about 250 to 300 feet..... No. 2 ...the field adjacent to the Red House. This site is even better for obtaining a rather larger quantity of water. No. 3 is smaller.... and the depth is greater. We should pass over this for the next site. No. 4 is one of the best supplies of water located. There are at least two strata......There is water here as near as 50ft from the surface; another strata at something over 100ft, ...The total yield is approximately 150,000 gallons per day. No. 5 is in all respects the same....but we believe this to be a distinct and separate supply from No. 4. Either or both of these latter sites can be obtained in the Garden, No. 657. No. 6 is a smaller supply located in the corner of the Kitchen Garden..... No. 7 is located below Strathculm House. The most suitable site for boring, is the corner of the Kitchen garden, the flow being towards the tennis court........'

It is a pity that the map identifying these sites was not attached to the report. The report continued with contractual details for the boring of a well should the Company choose to employ them.

'We should be prepared to enter into a Contract with you for this work irrespective of depth, and our estimated cost of the Bore in its entirety with the necessary steel linings would be Six hundred pounds.'

Patrick Hepburn, Director of Wiggins Teape replied on the 9th November 1927.

'We are much obliged by your of 5th giving a most interesting report of your visit. We have pleasure in enclosing our cheque for your fee, and the pleasure is increased by the fact that you use one of Wiggins Teape's papers for your report.   With reference to the suggested contract, we think that we could get a bore done for considerably less. .... .in your case a guarantee of 50,000 is so small as to be no temptation to us.'

On the 10th November 1927 there was a report on a small sheet of paper with three small sketches of sites for Boring on three additional pieces of paper. Beavis wrote on this page.
'No 1 is the strongest of the 3. No. 3 is stronger (if anything) than No. 2. Beavis 10/11/27.'
It is handwritten and at the bottom of the page and handwritten by another person, presumably someone in the Mill for Patrick Hepburn
'Mr. Beavis, water diviner, marked these plans shown on attached. He said there was "very strong" sign of water in garden behind rag boilers. This agrees with Mullins.'
Mr Beavis's favourite is interesting as it was in line with the large well in the back east entrance from Hele Road that then led into the old property known as Venmans. The land to the west, on which he drew his line as being 'anywhere on this line very strong', was the garden of Venmans. There were lilac and laburnum trees along the road edge, which remained until quite recently. The same entrance into the Mill still has the large well, but capped, and until recently was used as the central turning fixture for the large delivery lorries to manoeuvre around.

As to what was exactly carried out following those explorations is hard to define. The Mill had the large well already mentioned and maybe that was the Isler construction of a decade before. The Strathculm Well was constructed, with its reservoir higher in the field above it, in the first decade or up to 1913, and that supplied that property up Strathculm Road and other property down that road and in Hele Square, which were all owned by the Mill. The Mill also had agreement with Heale Payne, the farm close by, where it had the use of two wells on its land.

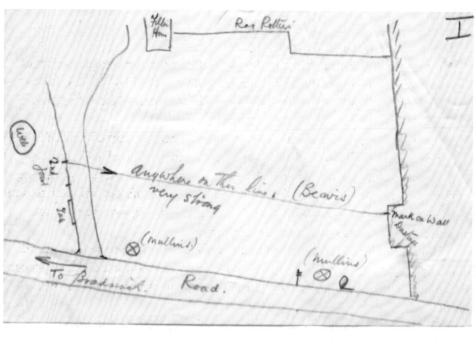

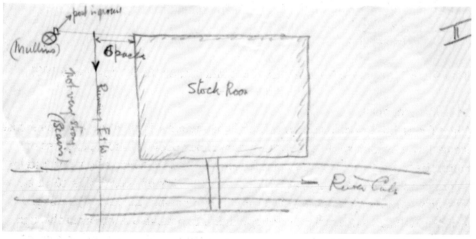

Illustrations of Beavis's water divining findings; nos. I and II sketches above; no. III on previous page.

Illustration of 1809 showing Copy Down springs, streams and Mills in item, page 54.

SECOND – COOMBE DRAINAGE.

There was correspondence about drainage at Coombe Farm, north of Hele Mills. The handwritten letters were of interest not only in their contents, but also in the style and method of communication. Each recorded acknowledgement at the top of the first page.

From the Duchy of Cornwall Office, Buckingham Gate, S. W. on the 11th January 1898.

'Dear Sirs,

      Coombe Farm, Bradninch.

     I duly received your letter of the 28th ult and observe your recital of the "history" of the laying of a drain about the year 1871 by Mr. C.R.Collins the then owner of Hele Mill with the consent of Mr. Anthony Martyn the then owner of Coombe Farm.

     Ths.H.Hepburn Esqr. to convey water from the wet part of a meadow on that farm for use at Hele Mill. In the deed of conveyance of 1876 by Mr. Martyn to the Duchy I do not find any reservation or declaration concerning the Grant of any water right such as you allude to. In the case of such Grants there is usually a document with the Title Deeds shewing whether it was a purchase for a Capital sum or for an annual rent.

     Would you kindly enquire of Mr. C.R.Collins whether he holds any such papers from Mr. Martyn? His papers or explanation would enable me to report intelligently on the subject and arrange for settling the question for the future.

     Mr. Martyn conveyed the property absolutely as free from any encumbrance or claim of right whatsoever.

       Yours truly
       G Herriot '

From Mr.A Martyn, Buckingham Lodge, Exmouth, on the 3rd April/May 1901.

'Dear Mr. Hepburn,

When I was the owner of Coombe I had the meadow in front of the Farmhouse drained at a considerable expense, it turned out useless, and a pure loss of money, because there was not a sufficient fall, this fall was only to be had by making a deep drain through Mr Collins' meadow, for of course this could be done only with his permission. The Tenant of Coombe (Mr Murch) arranged with Mr. Collins to drain the Coombe meadow and make a deep drain through his own meadow & at his sole cost – this was thoroughly done and as a great success. I do not remember of any repairs to the Drain being necessary, if there was Mr. Collins certainly did them. I may say that I entirely acquiesced in what my Tenant had done, and although there was no written Agreement between myself and Mr. Collins I should never have questioned his coming on the Coombe Meadows to repair the drain etc. If the Drain in his meadow came to be broken up the Coombe Meadow would become a swamp again in a year.   I remain,   Yours very truly,

> A.Martyn
> April / May 3rd 1901. '

From Mr. C R Collins, Hartwell House, Exeter, on the 4th May 1901 to T.H.Hepburn.

'Dear Hepburn

My recollection of draining the lower part of Coombe Farm Meadow in 1871 is that I was draining my own meadow, partly in the improvement and partly to increase the water supply to the Mill – I suggested to the then tenant of Coombe that it could be of great benefit to his meadow were I to drain it with my deep drains, he most gladly accepted my proposal with the result of a vast improvement of his swampy meadow & our increased supply of water to the Mill – of course from time to time the drain wanted looking to & I had perfect liberty to send and do what was necessary, & just mend on & no question raised and no written agreement made, for the good reason that the Coombe tenant & I there both benefited. I hope you still go on in the same way to the advantage of both

> Yours Sincerely
> C.R.Collins '

There is no final written outcome of the correspondence except that a typewritten letter from the Duchy of Cornwall Office in June 1911 to T.H.Hepburn Esq. refers to the same water meadows at Coombe.

'Sir,

Bradninch, Part Coombe Farm: Closes 12 & 769 (Ord)

Adverting to your conversations with Mr. Proudfoot with reference to the condition of the land drains in Closes 12 & 769 (Ord), I beg to inform you that there would be no objection, so far as the Duchy of Cornwall is concerned, to the Hele Paper Company entering upon these lands and repairing the drains, on the following conditions:-

(1) the work to be done to the satisfaction of the Duchy Land Steward;

(2) the tenant to be compensated for all surface damage;

(3) such permission to be without prejudice to the Duchy right to the entire control of the water.

> I am, Sir,
> Your obedient Servant,
> Walter Peacock '

Following are three illustrations of the first pages of the handwritten letters.

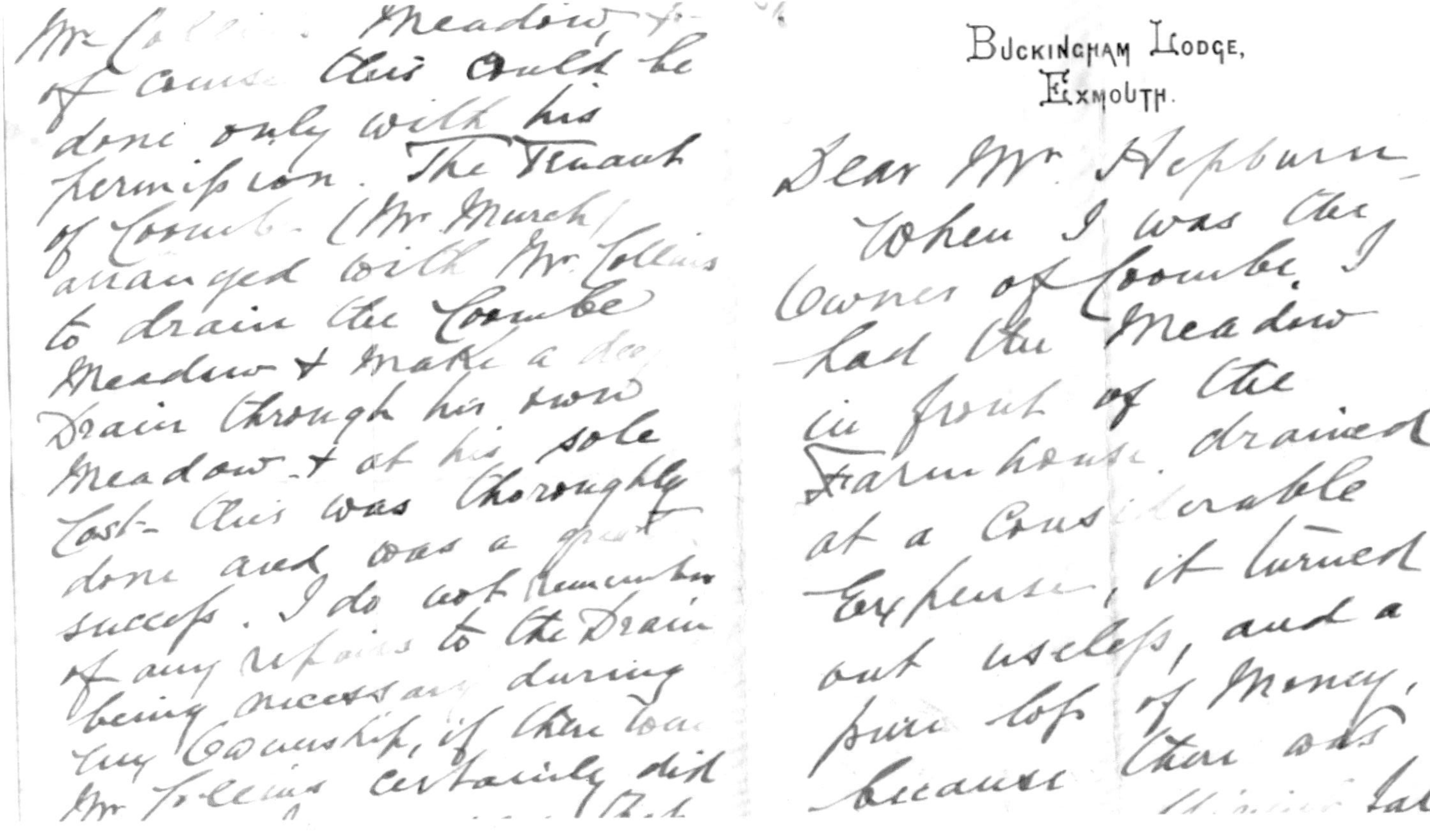

Dear Mr Hepburn

When I was the
owner of [...] Journal, I
had the [...] the Meadow
in front of [...] drained.
[...] farm house [...]
at a considerable
expense, it turned
out useless, and a
[...] out weeks [...] money,
[...] top of [...] was
because [...]

Mr [...] Meadow [...]
[...] could do his
[...] with his
[...]. The Viaduct
[...] ([Mr] Busch
[...] with Mr [...]
to drain the [...]
Meadow & make a [...]
Drain through his [...]
Meadow [...] at his sole
cost. This was thoroughly
done and was a great
success. I do not remember
any [...] to the Drain
[...] during
being [...], if there was
[...] certainly not
[...] [...]

Hartwell House,
Exeter. 4 May 1901

Dear Baptism

My recollection of mowing the lower land of Coombe Farm Meadow in 1871 no that was mowing my own meadow hardly for it improvement & hardly to increase the water supply for to mill — I suggested to him Jenard & I made that it need be & I made benefit to this Meadow now. It drew it into my next meadow to next of early

moving be accepted my proposal with the remit a vast improvement to render a vast improvement this Monday Meadow & our Monday Meadow is a greater supply of Water to

---

Duchy of Cornwall Office.
Buckingham Gate. S.W.

11th January 1898

Dear Sir,

Coombe Farm Bradninch.

I duly received your letter of the 28th ult. and observe your recital of the "history" of the laying of a drain about the year 1871 by Mr. C. R. Collins the then Owner of Hele Mill with the consent of Mr. Anthony Morphy the then Owner of Coombe Farm

THIRD – THE PROBLEMS OF FLOODS INTO THE MILL.

The landscape of the Culm Valley can tell you that millions of years ago the river had cut through the harder layers to form what we see today; a fairly wide flood plain with the river Culm winding its way down it to join the River Exe and on to the sea.

For the owners of the Hele Paper Mill however, a more local and present problem concerned them. Always the winter floods covered the whole valley floor due to high rainfall and water that came down the river from its source in the Blackdown Hills. The streams, some from local springs in the side hills, went into the river. One went directly through the Mill, so that in winter the Mill was again in the direct line for water to assault it.

The Mill also drew off a leat from the river, which took a channel of water right into the centre of the working areas. The Mill being alongside the river, should perhaps have been built on pillars, but it developed in a gradual way and maybe water didn't do so much damage when the equipment was less complicated.

The Mill was very much to blame for their problem of work being hindered and stopped and paper and equipment spoilt by getting flooded in most winters. They developed over the water meadows too much and constricted the natural waterways.

However it seems that in the nineteenth century there were other culprits. With the coming of the Railway through the West Country the Great Western Railway Company laid it down right through the length of the Culm Valley, following the line of the river. It was raised up on embankments over the worst of the marshy areas so it restricted the flood water to the central river line and thus caused that area to have deeper water levels in flood times instead of it spreading over a wider area.

The river area at Hele was at one of its narrowest in the length of the valley. At Hele things developed disastrously for the Mill as a road was built across the river and flood field. It linked the Hele village and Mill to the Railway and Station on the other side of the flood plain. It was built as a high causeway so that the road was, hopefully, high and dry. However, from letters written from the Mill in the twentieth century about the water tunnels under it being so very inadequate that the road ended under water at the highest flood times, it showed that mistakes of construction were identified.

On the 15th February 1923 J.P.Hepburn as Managing Director of Wiggins Teape the owners of the Paper Company at Hele Mill wrote to the County Surveyor. 'Dear Sir, About four years ago during the time of high floods, we took the difference in levels of the water on the upper and the lower side of the road between our Factory and Hele Station, and the difference was then 9"[inches] and we think Mr. Robinson, before he left drew your attention to our complaint. Last Saturday when we had a still higher flood, the difference in the centre of the roadway between the Mill and the Station was about 24" [inches] although nearer the bridge, just beyond our Factory, it was 18" [inches] thus showing that the roadway blocks the flow of water during high floods, and that a much larger opening is required in the roadway, so that the water may escape easily without causing the rush that it does. On the Siding which we have put over to our Factory the openings were quite large enough to let the water through easily, and if there had been a larger opening in the roadway there would be no cause for complaint.'

On the 9th March 1923 The Great Western Railway, Divisional Office at Taunton, wrote to Wiggins Teape at the Mill at Hele.
'Dear Sirs, Flooding at Hele. This Company's land was badly flooded during the recent heavy rains. As this has not happened previously, I have been making enquiries as to the cause and I find that the ditch alongside your field adjoining the Goods Yard at the Taunton end requires cleaning out. I am given to understand that your Company have tipped a lot of ashes close up to the hedge, with the result that some of the growth has been forced into the ditch. I have applied to Mr. Richards, of Poundapitt Farm, to have this ditch cleared but he has referred me to you. I should be obliged if you would have this clearing carried out without delay.'

In reply Mr. Hepburn on the 27th March informed the Great Western Company that he had arranged with Mr. Richards that the Mill would cut down their side and then the Farmer would clear his stream. He continued
'The whole cause, however, in our opinion, of the flooding of your land is owing to the openings in the road between our Factory and Hele Station not being large enough, and from particulars which were taken when the flood was at its highest we find that the level of the water on the upper side of the road was 18"/24" [inches] higher than on the lower side, thus showing there is a great obstruction.'
He continues that he had approached the County Council considering
'we hold that it is their duty to prevent extra flooding on our land.' And asks the Railway Company to assist in that ' it is possible that a joint appeal might do some good.'

The Great Western Railway Company replied on 28 March 1923 saying that
'I have already pointed out to the County Surveyor that the culvert to the public road near our Station appears to be inadequate to take the flood water.'

A handwritten note was dated 1 Aug 1923 and headed 'Road at Hele.'
'J.P.H., Mr. Simpson, Mr Cosway (assis. Surveyor) & Mr. T Lake (C.C. Bridges & Roads) looked at both walls 1-8-23. Mr. Simpson thought the C.C. should appoint a committee to examine & report, & that rebuilding of the walls is necessary. J.P.H. said that now was the time to approach the G.W.R. who would probably pay towards a culvert & J.P.H. said that W.T. & Co. would probably pay towards it. Simpson thought that enlarging the ditches on lower

side and thus making openings of present culverts more effective would do good. If nothing is heard in a month or two we should remind Mr. Simpson. Mr. Simpson agreed that a larger culvert or opening would do good.'

[J.P.H. stands for John Patrick Hepburn, then Manager of the Paper Mill; W.T & Co. stands for Wiggins Teape, the owners of the Paper Mill; C.C. stands for County Council; G.W.R. stands for Great Western Railway.]

A second handwritten note was dated 24.7.23 and headed

'Road from Station to Hele Mill'.

'The fence is broken on left hand side and is lying over at a pretty acute angle, and the wall needs several buttresses to keep it from going over further.'

It would look as though nothing was done about the small culvert under the road at that time, or if so it had not resolved the problem. Two handwritten notes on the Mill's headed Primrose paper in 1929 give us more information on water levels during high floods.

The first is dated 25th November 1929, and headed 'River Culm.'

'On the above date the difference in level above and below the main road between Hele and the G.W.R. station of Hele and Bradninch was measured. The water was found to be, on an average 12½ inches higher above than below the road. The points chosen for measurement were at the end of the bridge and just above the culvert near our bank level. These measurements were carried out and witnessed by John Ewart (Engineer) and W.Fry.'

A small diagram showing these points was added below.

The second is dated 28th November 1929, and headed 'R. Culm.'

'On the above date the difference in level above and below the main road between Hele and the G.W.R. Station of Hele and Bradninch was measured. The water was found to be six inches higher above than below the road. The point chosen for measurement was midway between the two culverts. This measurement was carried out and witnessed by the following - H.Richardson, John Ewart (Engineer) and W.Fry.'

The year 2002 saw a very high flood so it still goes on. The road was broken up through the violence of the water pouring across it. The Public House across the Railway got flooded as well as the Mill, which was forced to stop production. There are two largish tunnel culverts 9ft x 3ft and 6ft x 3ft under the road. Next to each one is a small round tunnel about 18 inches diameter. So at some time the smaller tunnel ones have been added to, but the problem must have continued as there were records by people alive today of vast flooding of the river valley at Hele throughout the second half of the twentieth century. Following the flood in the twenty-first century, major clearance of banks and ditches and the lowering of the Weir structure was undertaken by Mead, the current owners, in 2003/4.

Illustrations on the next page are of the water system under the Station Road causeway. Following page: Floods on 1st October 1960. Original from Rodney Goff. (also in 'Portrait of Bradninch' by Anthony Taylor). Next page: Floods in February 2003 across Station Road.

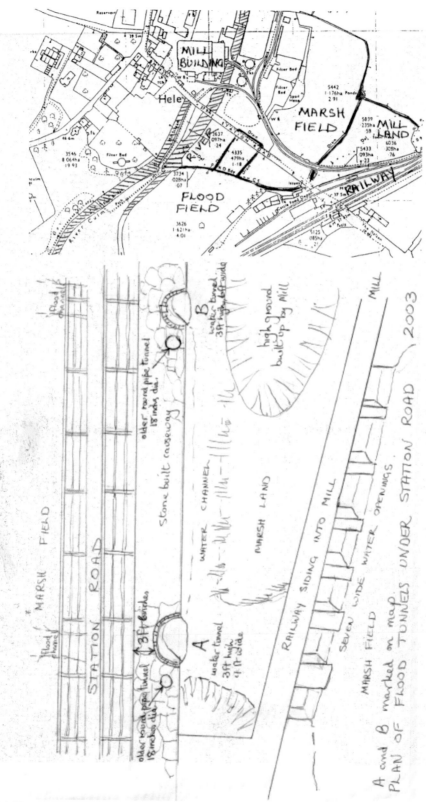

A and B marked on map.
PLAN OF FLOOD TUNNELS UNDER STATION ROAD   2003

A SECRETARY FOR ALL TIME; 1975-1994 – MEMORIES OF RENE PRING.

When I left school very many of the other girls at that time went into the Paper Mill at Hele, straight from school to work in the offices there. There were several departments and they learnt the skills and qualifications as they went along. Some, of course found employment in the Salle. I did not want to do that. I lived in Bradninch and it seemed too close and settled, so I went to college to learn secretarial and bookkeeping skills in Exeter. I then had a job in an office in Exeter for a few years before moving to work for Devon County Council who were starting a new County Supplies Department and I worked as secretary to the Head of Department and was involved in the organisation of all supplies for schools, residential homes, etc. I continued there for ten years, during which time I was married, and left when I started a family. As the children grew up I fancied some new work.

I became Clerk to the Bradninch Parish Council (now Town Council) which was a very convenient situation because we lived in the town; or rather from 1951 we were very high above it at the top of Beacon Hill. What a view! All the way to Dartmoor and the estuary and sea at Exmouth, even seeing the ships out to sea. We are still there in the same house on the hill. I was ready for more work so had part-time positions in Tiverton and Exeter before seeing an advertisement for secretary to the Mill Manager at Devon Valley Mill at Hele, but hesitated to apply as I didn't really want full-time work. However as it was near home I applied as my two sons had got past their early years, and was offered the position.

I now have to say I stayed until I retired ten years ago. And believe it or not I worked for seven different Managers, as they followed one after another. They held the number one job in the Mill for varying lengths of time and some moved on with increased position to other Mills or manufacturing businesses. Towards the end they were younger than me and perhaps I mothered them a bit for everyone always seemed to be sent to me if there was something wanted to be known that had happened in the past.

To start at the beginning; it was Jim Burnett who was Mill Manager that took me on. It was a strange ending to his time there, and remember I was new and didn't know too much of the business of making a profit from papermaking; but one day some-one 'high up' came down from Wiggins Teape's head office in Basingstoke and was in Jim Burnett's office with him. He had to leave his job and later I learnt that the latest new production line had not been a success and it was down to the Manager to shoulder the responsibility. That was quite an event but in general there were much quieter times and civilised departures of later Managers.

My second boss was Eric Dunmore, and he came up from Wiggins Teape's Mill in Ivybridge, near Plymouth to follow Jim Burnett. He was followed by Pat Harris, who was there quite some time. He was not a practical papermaker but did know the organisation of the business and how to get along with the workforce.

In 1984 Wiggins Teape relocated the Sales and Marketing Department from Head Office in Basingstoke to Devon Valley Mill at Hele, and Terry Coffey headed the new department as Marketing Manager. As additional office space was required for this it resulted in the taking over of the house, Ringmer, in which Mr. and Mrs. Passmore lived. Mr. Passmore had retired after working in the Mill all his life and had assumed he would spend his retirement in his own house. It was a sad and difficult task to help him accept a move to a house bought for him in Bradninch.

My early years saw me getting to know the ropes. Once when there were some Directors down from Head Office I was asked to take their car and get it filled with petrol prior to them going. I went off to the car park and found it was an automatic engine so in trepidation I drove it slowly and tried not to think of gear changing, through Bradninch, and was very glad to get back with it without incident or telling the Boss that I hadn't thought I could do it.
Another time there was the need to pick up an important visitor from Clyst St Mary and the company car was being used so I was asked if I'd drive over and pick up the Visitor in my own car. It was a small car and not particularly clean, but not to worry about that I was told. I arrived and the person was informed 'The car is here' and there I was as the driver and in my little Metro car, but as it turned out he was so relaxed and easy he sat in the front and chatted all the way over to Hele. I found out that he was a really important business-man, the Chairman of the London and Manchester Insurance Company. Mainly however I was busy in my own office seeing to the Manager's work.
A funny incident was talked about in the Offices and Mill as one day the Mill Manager (of the time, no name mentioned) while going through the Mill found a man sitting down reading a newspaper and was quite put out that he didn't jump up and get to work; so he told him to, only to discover he was a lorry driver waiting for his lorry to be loaded. Know your own men!

To continue on my list of Bosses. Jess Jarvis followed Pat Harris, and was also a very good Manager. When Jess Jarvis moved, Terry Coffey was promoted to General Manager. He and my husband, Basil, got along fine as my husband was still in aviation following on from his service as a pilot in the R.A.F. Terry Coffey had also done some flying and he and his wife, Maureen, remained good friends with Basil and myself.
WigginsTteape sold Devon Valley Mill to J.Bibby & Sons PLC in 1987 and the Mill was renamed Devon Valley Industries Limited. The change of ownership created a lot of additional work at the time.
One of my annual jobs was organising the Pensioners' summer outing. There would be a coach-full and we had a coffee stop, lunch at a Hotel, and afternoon and tea, usually at a seaside destination. This ended when we were taken over by Bibby as they had no pensioners! Another annual job was organising a Christmas Party for all employees with guests and this would be for about 350 people. Coaches with pick-up points all around the area was nightmare to arrange.

My next boss after Terry Coffey was Jeremy Bazley and at the time this came as a surprise because he was so young, about the same age as one of my sons, so this is where the mothering came in. Jeremy was working in the Bibby's Rochdale Mill. He had a local background from Silverton and had learnt papermaking at Bridge

Mill. (Silverton Mill), and had a solid knowledge of the paper industry. He was a hard working General Manager and Peter McLaverty was appointed as Mill Manager. After a few years Jeremy was appointed Divisional Manager, which encompassed the other Bibby mills. He moved his office to the closed Social Club which was located in the car-park.

Peter McLaverty took over as General Manager from Jeremy Bazley, but a Mill Manager was not appointed for a short time until the arrival of Garry Heap to fill the position. Peter was my last boss, the last of the seven names, as I retired in 1994, after nineteen and a half years at the Mill. It turned out I did spend most of my working life with papermaking and thoroughly enjoyed it.

I had a special leaving Dinner given to me and Basil at Combe House, Gittisham, with the Management team of Jeremy, Peter and Garry with their wives. They gave me a watercolour painting, commissioned especially, of the panoramic view from below my home on Beacon Hill above Bradninch. Two members from Head Office with their wives came down to join us. From the Mill I was given a very nice set of garden furniture.

There have been many changes in the Mill since I left.

There had been family links with Hele Mill in the past as my Mother worked there for 32 years. She was mainly in the Salle, but during the Second World War had worked on the Guillotine machine which in normal times was a man's job. She had to work shift-work but women were not allowed to do night-work. My Father was away in the Army at the time. Ruby Abrahams had worked alongside her on that job and her husband was also away at War. Ivy Tett also did the same job. Going back further Basil's Great Grandfather worked in the local paper industry and lost an arm in the machinery. His Grandparents also worked in both paper mills at Kensham, Bradninch, and after returning from serving in World War One his Father worked in the paper industry for the rest of his life.

After leaving school Basil joined the R.A.F. for pilot training in 1942 but was sent home to await an initial training course. During that time he spent nearly a year working in the Mechanic's Shop in the Mill at Hele. He was then recalled for permanent service and continued in military and civil aviation until 1990, so he did not return to the Mill.

Illustrations on following page are of Rene at her retirement on the 30th September 1994. Above: in her Office. Below: with Garry Heap and Peter McLaverty.

KICKING ADOUT IN HELE – MEMORIES OF ROBERT GITSHAM.

I loved the move to Number Two Station Road in Hele in about 1967.   It was right in the centre of the village exactly opposite the Lodge Entry of the Paper Mill in which my Father worked.   I was eleven at the time, in my first year at Broadclyst School, I had to tell them of my change of address.   We had lived all my earlier life at Parkview Cottages; they were four cottages along the road to Silverton Mill near Worth.   They were quite small and isolated except for three cottages near called Sunnyside.   For me there was no one to play with much; my brother, Chris, was quite a bit older and it was nearly a mile to walk to Hele.   Of course I did have good times there, in the 1962/3 winter, it was exceptionally cold with heavy snowdrifts.   I went tobogganing on the hill above Worth Farm.   There was fun also down on the Bye river when the ice was breaking up except one time; I was with Chris and his friend while they were throwing lumps of ice back onto the half frozen river and somehow I fell onto a large floe and it went down the river.   I was heading for the concrete bridge and beyond that the ice was solid apparently.   They raced to the bridge and grabbed me when I got there otherwise I would have gone under it and under the solid ice beyond.   I don't remember the incident but Chris said it gave him the fright of his life as he was looking after me and he said he never told Mum and Dad.

We used to go as far as Silverton Mill and once saw a pair of swans take off in tandem, there near the bridge.   The wingspan of the two was amazing and they ran on the water side by side to get airborne.   Chris shouted at me to get away thinking they were coming for us, but I was mesmerised by them and anyway I had no fear of them, they were going up the open water.   Today the river is different, it is overgrown on the banks and shallow with a lot of the open clear stretches lost.

It was always the field and river way as the best to get to Hele.   There was an iron girder-type aqueduct across the river that we used, then past the railway bridge opposite Clyst Hayes which we called Black Bridge, as it was black coloured, under the railway flood bridge, over the river again at Green Bridge, so named as the handrails were painted that colour, we were very imaginative in our names! through the wooded area up to The Lodge, where Pete lived, and then down Strathculm Road.   Hele Square was good with the little shop and Post Office that Miss Andress kept.   The buses, both to Cullompton and to Exeter stopped outside the Mill.   And in Hele there were others to play with just on my doorstep.   There was Pete Lush up at The Lodge, Binney Brady in the Square, Joff Wykes up Waterworks Lane, and later John Nash when he moved into Hele in 1970.

I knew all the countryside, and loved fishing.   Sometimes there were four of us boys sitting on the aqueduct fishing, cursing the pike as they caught so many fish and even leapt up and grabbed them off our hook.   I tried to catch pike but they are hard to get.   There was a lot of fishing on that stretch, with competitions on Sundays with licences from the Exonian Fishing Organization.   Coaches came out from Exeter to park at Beare for the day.   Fishermen went down the track, over Bye River, and had staked out sections between Silverton Mill and Black Bridge. Asked what was Bye River and that was the name we had for the river that left

Hele at the Weir and rejoined it at Beare. I knew the workings of the Mill quite a bit, I was interested in it all, so knew about the Weir and Bye River. My father told me that in the distant past earlier in the century, the Weir was shut at times in the summer so the main Culm river went down the Bye; it was then held back further along to flood the fields to irrigate them. Better grass for the cows in the late summer and the aqueduct took water across above the Culm to the field on the other side. At those times only the Leat water going through the Mill which went out below the weir keep the Culm flowing down the next stretch, until the Bye rejoined it. It ran very low at those times, and not too pure either.

As I grew up I was interested in a lot of the local sports. There were many activities from the Mill and workers belonged to various teams. The most successful was football. Devon Valley Football Club was to be reckoned with. They played on the field of Hele Payne across from the Mill. All teams had comfortable changing areas in the Mill with plenty of hot water and the canteen there. At one time the Youth team of Bradninch had some good players and they went into the Devon Valley team and the team went right up the league to be a top team. It included Roy Nott, Peter Lush, Rodney Goff, Ken Salter and Reg Palfrey. One player, Kenny Freeman, whose father Cliff worked in the Mill went on to play for Elmore in Tiverton and later became their Manager. Of course us younger boys just played our 'kick abouts' in Big Field up Strathculm Road.

I believe there was earlier interest in Tug of war competition and they used the lone oak tree in the Station Road field to practise against; and they also used a forty gallon oil drum filled with concrete.

There was no special cricket team linked to the Mill, local men played up in Bradninch but a really big interest was Athletics, especially running. Father was a good runner and there was a group of them. They were keen on middle distance but did some marathon style events. I went to one in a Youth event to run from Bampton to Tiverton but didn't know where exactly the finish post was; but we all got there in the end. Father often practised and ran on a grass track and achieved a four minute ten second mile once; and that was before the war. With him usually were his brother Len and Archie Ellicott. There was a gap in time before there became an interest in running at the Mill again, but a later running team included Dave Smith, Ian Kerrick, Alan Luke, Roger Nicolas and Chris Abrahams. They used to train from the Mill around the roads there. I expect they were glad to be out in the fresh air and the countryside after a long shift. I used to wait at my gate for them to go by, if I followed as they went along Station Road I was left behind before they got to Hele Cross. Later when I owned the Butcher's business in Bradninch Dave Smith told me he used to train by starting there and going on several circuits up Beacon Road and back round at fifteen minutes each time.

When I was young I played football for the under fourteens in Broadclyst on a Saturday. I used to leave the home, No. 2 Station Road, with my boots tied around my neck and instead of catching the bus, I would go down the Drive, over the weir, across the field, under the railway, over the concrete bridge over the Bye river and on to Beare which was on the main road. I caught the bus from there and the fare was 3d instead of the 6d from Hele. I therefore had three pence to buy a fizzy drink. My Dad told me many years later that I ran so well and fast on that route I would have made a good cross country runner. The other boys and I had many meeting places around the village. We were often in the woodland next to the Lodge as it belonged to the Mill but no one looked after it that much. The great Sequoia redwood tree we called the Jobby tree as we pulled off bits of bark, which did the job of starting our camp fires as it was ideal for that. I could create the noise of the female owl by whistling through my thumbs; we would wait a bit and then the male owl would start screeching his own sound. Nearby was a huge beech, which was ideal for a few initials to be carved on it. Some still there I am told. Another tree was called Jackdoor and another Den tree as it was perfect to just climb up and there was a centre that we could all sit in, and of course the special tree in the middle of Big Field was called Conker tree for obvious reasons. Our favourite activity was always kicking around. We used to play footy outside the double gates at the Lodge, they were set back a little way from the road and made an ideal goal for shooting practice. As Pete lived there it was alright and especially when his Mum and Dad went out every Saturday night without fail to Bingo in Bradninch. When we had a new type football made of the hexagonal patches there was a disaster as it went over the gates, which often happened but with that new ball it curved and went straight into the slit window of the Lodge. It broke the glass and we had to wait and confess when they arrived home. We were told we couldn't play football there anymore and someone came up from the Mill and mended the window. Of course us boys said to each other it had never happened before except that once, so it won't again, so the very next Saturday we were there and exactly the same thing happened because although we did not realise it, the new ball was faster and it took a twist to it in mid air. That was a bad evening to have to confess a broken window again. After that we never played into the gates again but used the narrow opening that led into the wooded part up to the Waterworks further up Strathculm Road. That proved very good for our skills as it was so narrow we just had to kick the ball well to get it in.

On other Saturday nights in the winter we would first go to the pub, The Railway Hotel, that was in Hele. We took a flagon to the bottle and jug door and Mr. Baker would fill it up with shandy. He said that was alright for us, so then we went back to the Lodge to play cards and of course we knew Pete's parents came home on the eleven bus after Bingo so finished and went home before that. We could raise a bit of pocket money by collecting empty beer bottles along the railway line. These were thrown out from trains and Mr. Baker gave us the refund money on them. There were good social and fun events connected to the Mill for the workers. Most outings were linked to sports meetings but we kids did get given a Christmas party in the Guildhall with lots of food and a present from Rodney Goff 'Santa'.

So my time in Hele was good, and I then trained to become a Chef, and with that skill, I travelled the world quite a bit you could say. All sports interested me, and when I first went up to London to continue my training after College in Exeter I saw information about Cassius Clay being in the city. He was there on a promotion and photographic session prior to a match. I went along and watched him doing a training session of boxing. I got his autograph on a newspaper cutting of him and I got several other well-known names.

After London I worked on a luxury yacht in the Mediterranean for some time. That was well paid so I left that with plenty of money in my back-pocket. Sport had a hand in things again as following a sporting tour in the U.S.A. I went back to South Carolina to work as a Chef for five years before returning to live in Bradninch.

My father started work at the age of fourteen, in Exeter for a Foundry firm, feeding the fire with coke. He had to help his family with wages so on a Saturday had a second job as a butcher's boy in Pinhoe; helped to kill and cure the pigs brought in, then later in the day became the delivery boy and had to ride a horse bare-back with just the bridle to control it and the basket of meat on his arm. It was a sensible horse and my Dad was supposed to only trot it on the roads to the outlying villages, but young-like, once around the corner he speeded it up quite a bit. He was born and brought up in Broadclyst, had no connection with Papermaking but was taken on at Hele when he was sixteen. This was an achievement as he had no previous family connection, which was what usually counted, but they checked what and where his father and grandfather worked. He started as the Lodge Boy. He had to run errands etc. and they had working horses so when they went out and up to the waterworks he had to go too; to immediately collect their droppings from the road, which had to be put on the rose beds in the Mill.

He went on to be Stoker/Boilerman. At first there were three boilers in the Boilerhouse, they were like three steam engines. Twelve-hour shifts were endless shovelling coke to all three. Later the huge concrete Boilerhouse was constructed with first of all a concrete floor over the old boilers. That was in the 1950's and the new furnace, from Gateshead, put on the new floor. The old boilers were used right through the construction and most likely still there like old forgotten monsters. The new furnace had a conveyor system for fuel to feed it. There were levers to control the speed of the conveyor belt and others to regulate the air into the furnace and the clinkers fell through to the floor below. The steam produced was piped to the three paper machines and was used to dry the wet material at the finish end. So the pressure gauges for all three were constantly being checked and speed of fuel and air altered as to requirements from the Papermachinemen. The wrong steam supply and the paper was not running off the end in the right dry condition and so ruined. If there was too much pressure it had to be let off and also to lose heat in the furnace; so anyone could see it happening as black smoke would pour out of the tall Mill chimney; but very rare if my Dad was in charge. I used to take my Dad his Sunday lunch, just go across the road with a hot meal on a plate; it was more open and easy in those days. I would check the gauges for him while he had his meal.

The fuel went into the Mill by trucks on the railway siding right close to the Boilerhouse. One man, who had to be small sat up on the gantry in a small wire box cage and he would scoop the coke out of the truck and onto the pile in the Mill. I can visualise him still perched high up there; I never knew his real name I only heard him called Tonto. It may be that later a hoist system was installed on the side of the Boilerhouse and the trucks were bodily lifted up and tipped so the fuel went inside.

My father had a long, hard, working life. To me, as a boy just kicking around in Hele, he was either on long shifts in the Mill, or he had to sleep at strange times in the day if he was on nights. Otherwise he was out working on our garden providing the vegetables for us. The garden was over the road to the house in the old Reservoir site on Hele Road. There were some wonderful fruit trees there, a large Bramley apple and pears that make my mouth water when I think about them.

The top illustration is of Bob's Dad, Reg Gitsham, (on the right) with his co-worker and friend Em Luke, outside the old Boilerhouse, in June 1939.
Below is of Bob Gitsham as a young boy at Parkview sledging above Worth in 1962/3.

The illustration above is of the construction of the new Boilerhouse in the late 1940's.
The illustration on page 162 is of the Presentation of long service awards at the Rougemont Hotel in Exeter in 1974.
A full list of recipients is in my first book 'Memories from the Mill' page 77: several familiar names are there, with Reg Gitsham (top right hand side) his brother, Leonard (just below); and including Violet Broom and Walter Wingrove who have items in this book.

Illustrations on this page of two Football Teams. (courtesy of the Bradninch Football Club)
Top: 1950/51 Cup Team, at Hele with Mill in background; standing from left; Ken Salter, Ted
Bowerman, W. Radford, R McArdle, S Holmes, R Greening, S Gillard, Ron Salter, Les Turner.
kneeling in front; A Maidment, W Wingrove, C Freeman, W Hancock, D Thomas.
Bottom: Youth Team, approx.1968/70. back row; E Bowerman, K Freeman, D Retter, G Hancock,
N Meadows, P Meadows, J Cudmore. front row; J Huxtable, P Hawkins, R Nicholas, J Wingrove,
C Wykes, M Brady.

THE MILL IN THE LAST DECADES OF THE TWENTIETH CENTURY – MEMORIES OF MERVYN CLARKE.

In this year of 2004 I will be having my fiftieth birthday. I work at the Paper Mill in Hele and it is in this year, a few months ago, that there has been yet another change of ownership. I started work there thirty years ago when I was young, just aged twenty. People told me at the time I wouldn't like it and wouldn't want to stay. This was because I had lived all my life up until then on farms and was working since leaving school at Park Farm in Bradninch. I had been born at one of the pair of farm cottages above Bradninch at Foreward Green; my parents moved in when they were first built; our one for the farm where my father worked down towards Hen Street.

Unfortunately he died when I was two so I don't recall any of that but we, my Mother, older sister, Sandra, and me moved to a Duchy cottage near Park Farm a few years later because the other farm needed to give the Foreward cottage to the new farm-worker when he married. So I was working on the farm until I was twenty but I did not like it much, I found it a lonely life.

On one of my breaks at the farm I walked down to the Mill a mile or so away and asked to see if I could work there. The Personnel Manager saw me although they first of all said I would need an appointment. He took me into the huge Machine Room and it just seemed enormous and the papermaking machine went on forever. He said that would be where I would work. I decided to have a go! Friends said I wouldn't like it, so different to my outdoor farming job, but I thought if I didn't like it, well in a year I would be old enough to train to get an H G V Driving Licence and that could be a good job. It worked out well as I am still there.

The main thing about the working, especially from the start, was the shift pattern. There was a Foreman in charge of a shift and you were a member of that group. What he was like was important and how he ran things and looked after you. When I started our Foreman was in charge of two machines so he had about twenty men under him because there were three men to each machine, and also the pulping and mixing and the cutting and trimming. The finishing, counting and packing, if it was a night shift, was left for the day shift of women who came in to do that. So that at night it was just us getting on with making the paper, unless the machine broke down and then the Foreman would have to call in the Engineer. Of course later there was always more machinery brought in and used such as to cut and count the sheets; and then later still the paper was completed in its roll off the machines and sent to the customers packaged that way to be processed on by the various companies that bought our paper.

Once a year in the Autumn, it was Housekeeping Week. The place got cleaned and sorted out and we got our new safety boots; no other clothes or equipment, only boots. There was competition between the machine shifts as to the award for best housekeeping, and there were usually a couple of open evenings for families and visitors to go round.

I had a good Foreman for some time in that he seemed to get us any perks such as diaries that were handed out. Otherwise we were often forgotten by the Staff members. He also organised us into a good team for out of work activities such as skittles, darts, quizzes, evenings and pub visits out. There were sport and social events in the Autumn. We went up in coaches, usually two, to Glory Mill, which was in Buckinghamshire and was part of the Wiggins Teape Company that owned Hele. They had all the facilities there and we joined in the sporting competitions. They were great days out with one coach coming straight home with families and the second coach stopping for us to have a meal on the way back. Maybe our visits there got people thinking that we needed more in Hele; anyway they cleaned up the tennis court along the river and we played there for about three years. Then they planned to build a social club at the end of the car park that had come into being after the demolition of the houses in Hele Square. We missed the small shop there as when I started, and later, the youngest member of the shift during the day, was always sent out to get snacks, drinks and fags for the whole shift.

The Mill management and a local Brewery firm put up the money for the social club but the men did some of the work. After a shift I would put in an hour or so with first the digging out for the foundations and the laying the concrete floor. There was no machinery so it was hand labour. The building was pre-fabricated and was erected I presume by the firm because I next put in some time on the internal decorations. It was a good venue for meeting up with friends and to have a few beers, which were cheaper than in a pub, and we had several skittle teams within the workers of the Mill and quizzes and bingo sessions for those that liked that. It did fail some years later when the Mill was owned by a different firm who maybe weren't so supportive of extra things outside production of paper. Also with more workers living all over the area and quite a few from Exeter; in fact after I was married I lived in Exeter and drove to work by car; so the drink/drive legislation kept people away from drinking in Hele and then driving home. Previously it would have just been a bike ride up to Bradninch for most employees. In the Mill itself there was a very good canteen with meals cooked there for you. It was great to come off shift to a Big Breakfast for 10 pence (and that old money) and with beans and tomatoes it went up to 12 pence! Like everything in industry changes occurred to streamline or economise; food was in cabinets for us to microwave, no friendly lady cook to add an item to your plate; and now it's only packaged sandwiches and snacks.

So we have seen a lot of changes during the last thirty years at the Paper Mill. With Wiggins Teape coming to an end as owners it seemed to bring in changing work attitudes to us employees. The Mill was bought by B.A.T. (British American Tobacco Company) and some things worked out good to be with an International Company. More organization developed from Hele rather than orders and plans sent down from Head Office as before with Wiggins Teape. Also they offered the employees shares in their company and many in Hele took that up. I did and you chose a save as you earn way to pay for shares bought for you at special low rate and realised five years later when they were sold for you. It was a good scheme and although my shares had to be sold on a specific day and that unfortunately was the famous Black Monday on the stock exchange so I didn't get as much as I would have done if sold on the day before; I could pay off my mortgage on my house with that windfall.

Later Bibbys, and then Barlow owned the Mill before we became part of the American Paper Empire of Mead. With Wiggins Teape the paper for filters for the motor industry was sent to a sister company to be impregnated with suitable chemicals but afterwards an Impregnator machine was installed at Hele. I moved over to work on it and it was a difficult process as it was not possible to do that process within the paper production in the papermaking machine. The paper had been dried and now had to be worked wet again to absorb the chemicals and also once through the Impregnator the paper could not, if spoiled, be recycled again. All waste was unusable and especially at the start there were skips and skips of waste. With ordinary papermaking we always said for some unknown reason we produced better paper from recycled waste from the machine.

The other cost with taking on the impregnation work was that the rolls of paper had to be full or at least half size to go on the rollers, but customers bought it in odd sizes and in small quantities. We had a store-room for the finished rolls and it ended up with one employee working out the most economical way to deal with each order, and at times they got fed up with it and started on a fresh roll. That made me realise why previously the company who did it before bought so much paper from us while less was sold on. Another risk with the process was that the chemicals were highly inflammable. We were classified as the second highest risk in the area and any hint of a possible fire in the Mill set off three fire engines to come, each from a different station and each to follow different routes to us.

With Mead there was a sense that there was a cultural divide between their way of working and the British way. They expected us to accept being laid off and on as it suited the orders and it seemed to me that they put their American interest first; often moving our orders over there and also having bought our skills could transfer those papermaking skills over to their machines over there. We were left with very little and downgraded all the time. Perhaps expendable in the end.

This year however the Mill has not been closed down, it has in truth too good a history and too much good machinery not to survive the economical bad times it sometimes goes through. We are now owned by a long-standing British papermaking Company, J.R.Crompton. There seems to be a sense that I have come full circle again to when I started. This firm has a head office and Paper Mill in Manchester so all the running of the business at Hele has gone up to there. They also have a Paper Mill in Gloucester. The products are paper specialised for the food industry, such as filter paper for teabags, for containing cold meats and maybe soon filter paper for coffee. Buying another site, Hele, with another machine as security of continuous supply secured exclusive orders for those products. Crompton have set up our machines with tight quality controls; as for example it marks the line of paper through the machine as soon as the smallest fault is detected and then we have to stop and go back, rejoin, and start up again. Also there is a lot of time spent testing and retesting the pulp to match it exactly each time. By comparison, we produce the rolls of paper in very quick time once we are given permission to be up and running. There seems a future in this new area of the market and Hele has the machines to do it and I hope we continue for at least as long as I personally want to work there. On the wider view it would be a shame if that Paper Mill at Hele should ever have to close down.

Illustration at top: M.P. Angela Browning with Managing Director, Jeremy Bazley meeting Mervyn in Machine Room in 1992. below: Social Club built at end of Mill carpark.1980's.
Following page: at top: Machine No.2, photograph taken in 1985. below: New machine No.5, photograph taken in 2002.

166

WAGGONERS – DECADES INTO THE PAST.
Memories from DAVID LAND and STELLA and LES VALENTINE.

All through the compilation of this second collection of memories and items of historical interest linked to Hele some new information has emerged that linked into items in my first collection 'Memories from the Mill'. One area that had been sparse on continuity was the use of horses in the Mill and the men who worked with them. Luckily more has now come to light.

David Land's great grandfather was Giles Maddock. His name has cropped up in connection with horses. He was on the 1891 census as living in Hele, aged 35 with employment as a Waggoner. His wife was Sarah, aged 28, and was a Paper Sorter in the Mill. They had one child, Eliza, aged 2, at home and also in the household, Elizabeth Griffin, aged 22, the sister of Sarah, as lodger and a Paper Sorter. Giles Maddock, his wife and Eliza, with a younger daughter, Bessie, aged 4, were still there on the 1901 census. There had been two older children, John, born 1883, and Emma born 1886 but they both died within four days of each other in early childhood; Emma on 23rd October 1887, John on 27th October 1887 which must have been a very sad time for the Maddocks.

David Land has records of the family from the marriage of Giles to Sarah Jane Griffin. The family lived at the corner house of Station Road and Strathculm Road (now called Mews Cottage and an item about it in my first book, page 47). In the Maddock time it was a house at the entrance end on Station Road, with the second part as stables for two horses. The cobbled drive was there with the outbuildings and hayloft. The house was called Rose Villa; a flower name to link to Mill properties Rose Bungalow and Clematis Bungalow in Strathculm Road.

Eliza, the third child, born 1889, married John Hodge Land and moved away to Tiverton and among their descendants is David Land. He has two photographs from the past in Hele; one of Bessie, the second daughter, now grown up and with her father, Giles in the garden of Rose Villa; and the second one sitting behind her husband on a motorbike in front of Rose Villa just in the entrance from Station Road. Bessie married Ernest John Miller, another family name involved in the Mill. They lived on in Hele, he worked on the Paper Machines and she was a Paper Sorter in Silverton Mill. Everyone walked to work then and thus she did the mile and a half both ways. They had no children and unfortunately he died of lung congestion from the paper dust, aged 46, and she died three years later.

The second memories, those of Stella and Les Valentine also link back to Giles Maddock. Stella's grandfather was Herbert Power; he was the Waggoner for some time at Hele Mill and most likely followed on from Giles Maddock. He was there in the 1930's as Walter Wingrove remembered him as working with the horses when he started in the Mill in 1932. (earlier item, page 56) Herbert married Florence (Florrie) Haydon whose family were connected with agriculture and they all emigrated to Canada except Florrie who remained with Herbert. They succeeded well out there, especially when oil was drilled from under their land. Herbert was renowned for his skill with horses and also hounds as he was, either before he worked in the Mill or alongside that work, the whipper-in for the local hunt. He rode the leading horse in the local carnival in fine clothes, the horse beribboned and even to carrying a live fox under his arm. A great showman on that occasion! The Power family lived in the corner house so Giles Maddock had moved away in old age or had died by then. Stella's father, Ralph Power followed his father into the Paper Mill at Hele but worked on the Papermaking machine. Stella, after leaving school also worked in Hele, but not in the Mill; she worked for Mr. Passmore, who was the Chief Accountant for the Mill, known by all as W.H. (his Christian name initials, believed to be William Henry). The Passmore family lived at Ringmer, in Station Road next to the Mill Offices. The daughter Pauline lived with her parents and worked in the offices in the Mill and Stella looked after her young son, Chris, from the age of six months for nine years; five at Ringmer and a further four in Exeter. When W.H. retired his nephew, Max Passmore, took over from him. W.H. lived to ninety years of age.

Stella knew most people in Hele and after her grandparents left the house on the corner (she doesn't recall it having any name, so the name Rose Villa must have been dropped by that time) a Mrs Thomas lived there with her daughter Grace. Grace never married and worked for the Mill Manager, Mr. Richardson.

Les Valentine's grandfather, Gilbert, was first cousin to Giles Maddock. Gilbert had three brothers, one emigrated to New Zealand, one to Canada to work on the Trans-continental railway but who died back in Europe in the First World War and the third, Alex, worked with Gilbert at Hele Paper Mill.

Les grew up at Ellerhayes, close to Hele. He started work as an apprentice carpenter with Nicks Builders in Bradninch and was paid 2/6d a week at the beginning. Nicks was a large builder's firm then employing something like 200 people, with 10 Joiners and 4 Machine-men in the carpenter's shop. The apprenticeship lasted many years in those days but eventually you were classed as a craftsman. Unfortunately Les suffered a spinal injury while serving in the Second World War so that working was not easy after that. He got employment at the Paper Mill in Hele in the Quality Control department, which lasted for 7 to 8 years and was then able to work again as a carpenter in the Mill for a further 21 years. He worked in the Mill buildings and also the Red House that the Manager lived in, and the new wooden Bungalow built in the gardens of Strathculm House for the Under Manager, Mr. Ruddick; but he was not part of the workforce who looked after the houses the Mill had for its workers. So Les had links to the Paper Mill during his working life, but not in any way linked to the horses.

Les remembers some good times while working and joined the gymnastics club in the Chapel Hall in the Hele Square; like Walter Wingrove (earlier item, page 51) he remember the man who ran it with the nick-name of Magic because he was so athletic and fit.

Illustrations on next page: top; Giles Maddock with daughter, Bessie. below; Bessie and Ernest on motorbike. date about 1920.
Ref: Pauline Passmore is in 1930 Staff photograph on page 83.
Ref: in first book 'Memories from the Mill' Item: Mews Cottage pages 47-49; Item: Hazel Rowland page 51, map page 55; Item Horses in the Mill page 69-74.
Adjustment: Illustration in first book, page 71, Almost certain this is of Giles Maddock leading the horse with Eliza, his daughter beside him. Correction: the name Mr. Powel should be Mr. Power.

170

Retirement Dinner for Bill Maddock and Ralph Power (51working years); 4th January 1969. standing from left: Roy Nott, Herbert Summers, Eric Clark, Eric Snell, Roy Norman, Colin Stoneman, Cyril Hobbs, Jack Rosser, Percy Budd, Walter Wingrove, Dia Davis, Dick Drew, Donald Pearce, George Cumming. seated from left: Fred Drew, Nat Baxstone, Sid Betts, Bill 'Ducky' Maddock, Ralph Power, Bob Paisley (Manager).

The laying of the Railway in the 1840's, and even more relevant, the creation of the road - STATION ROAD - that linked Hele village to it, had a huge effect on the natural river, streams and flood plain. It was constructed as a raised causeway with floodwater channels built under it.

I have to confess to some creative input as the documents and maps of earlier times were not as precise as the more recent Ordnance Surveys. The Tythe map of 1841 is quite detailed so that to overlay earlier maps onto this gives the long-term view before the building of the Station Road Causeway. The Surveyor's Drawings of 1796 and The Devon Book of Maps of 1809 give the layout of the hamlet of Hele with the buildings set together as a working centre. We see the natural intertwining of tracks and buildings. It gives the impression that people came and worked and lived in Hele right under the Mill; not to go there to pass through to other places. In Hele itself the road from Bradninch curved closer to the river and the Mill works because it went close into the old longhouse, called Venmans, that existed then at the back of the Mill. The entrance to the Mill was also a large wide opening curving in further along this road. Almost opposite was the entrance to the very old and much used track of Hilly Lane. Hilly Lane was never upgraded to a tarmac road and has degenerated in use and care until now it is a right of way footpath only. The road to Bradninch was altered greatly in the time after the production of the Tythe map. It was realigned straight right from the central junction cutting across the field or orchard on the farmland side. The entrance to the Mill was closed with a very high straight wall. The entrance to Venmans was moved further away from it into this straight road although it remained an entrance to that property and the Mill. Later on an avenue of London Plane trees were planted along this stretch of road and are today a unique and special feature, the pride of the hamlet.

The lane from Silverton came into the present centre as now, but was narrow between farm working buildings to the junction and the very old house on the corner was there, as was the Mill House opposite. The road to the river from the central junction went a little way along, as today, but then curved into the area westwards before it crossed it.

One can quite see the effect of the Railway and the Station Road as it still is today. The road was built straight from Hele across the river and direct to the Railway Station the other side of the flood fields. Immediately it made the whole area refocus on its needs and uses. The railway and the use of it at the Hele and Bradninch Station became a primary use. People from Bradninch went through the small settlement to reach the station. Goods and cattle were moved about from it through Hele. Station Road went on after the railway and so road routes were used through this settlement to other villages and farms on the other side of the valley. One does not imagine that people and carts, and horses etc. had not crossed the river valley at Hele before the coming of the railway but in studying earlier maps and looking on the ground itself it has to be assumed it was not an easy route. The Surveyor's Drawings of 1796 gives no doubt that a lane or track went from

Hele across the wetland. It was shown as leaving the hamlet to the south of the Mill so that on today's layout it would have crossed the river from the car-park area which was the old farm and tanyard property with the orchards around the settlement. After it crossed the marsh fields the track turned a loop as it reached the higher ground; it then curved towards the farmstead of Poundhayes, which has the name of Poundapit Farm today. It continued over the hills towards Clyst Hydon with a double junction one back towards Beare and the other to the farmstead of Potshayes. The one to Beare was on a line half-way up the hill on that side of the valley. On the ground at present can be seen the start of its line as a track leaving Beare and coming part way to a wooded area above Poundhayes. To walk it across the landscape is enthralling, following a level way over fields; old trees, bits of hedges and banks; to the remaining hedges, no double hedges left just on one side, then the other side, with present field gates set at right angles that would have been across the old road. The later constructed present main road links across lower down the hill, through the small wood of Woodhayes, to pass near Poundapit Farm and on to Cullompton.

The map of 1809 in the Book of Devon Maps gives us very similar information. It showed the hamlet of Hele and indicated the marshy land clearly.

Other maps that help are the Tythe Maps of 1841 of Broadclyst and Bradninch when seen together. The road from Hele to Poundapit Farm is shown on the same line as the earlier maps. There is difficulty in seeing the route actually crossing the River Culm as the Parish boundary is there and each Parish had its own map and ended at its boundary. However another map, the Deed Map of 1843, (shown fully in item 'The River Culm - Between Hele and Killerton, pages 74,75), clearly marks the road as 'from Heale' crossing the river. The route was the same as on the other maps in that it went into Hele at the farm and tanyard area, (present day car-park), with a second small track from the Mill that crossed the river into its adjacent land. The road route was shown as crossing onto the constructed spit of land, called The Avenue in Mill deeds, with the Mill Leat on the other side, and so the road route looks as though it went up The Avenue into the main centre of Hele close to the Mill and maybe not across the Leat into the orchard area of the farmstead and tanyard. When we come to the later construction of Station Road it crossed the river close to or on that other small Mill track. It did not wind down the spit of land to the old road route. The Ordnance Survey in the early twentieth century showed that new straight route.

What confuses the situation, in the present time, is that the parish boundary over the marsh land is the present-day stream running to the river in the place of the old road. Centuries ago the waterway was most likely a stream alongside the road. That old road has gone – lost through no longer being used; gone under the soil of today's water meadows, but the stream remains in its place. Some field names and ownerships on the Tythe Map are of interest. The enclosures under the name of 'Bindles' are identified on the map on page 185 in the item on that name. Likewise, land under Late Warrens in the Bradninch parish was identified in the first volume of historical items, page 144. The Mill at Hele, owner John Dewdney, also owned one field, no 277, in Broadclyst that was adjacent to the river at Hele, through which the new water-course of 1843 started from the river at Hele.

The three marsh areas were listed under 'Colly Marshes' as no.279, great colly marsh, no.280, middle colly marsh, no.281, little colly marsh. The owner of that land was Campion Richard Grudge esq. who also owned Poundapit; the occupier of both was Robert Pring.

The other fields linked to local names were under the title 'Germains', being no.278 little marsh, no.290, weaver marsh, no.285, lower spatland, and no.301, higher spatland. The owner occupier was Thomas Martin, whose name was recorded as involved with the paper mills in the Culm Valley.

Exploration on the ground raises some items of interest. On the west side of the present Station Road bridge over the river Culm at times of very low water there can be seen on the bed of the river a laid down stone straight track. It is constructed of square stone about a metre and a half wide with long thin edging stones. It came into view the summer after the river had been cleared of reeds and willows. It went to just over the centre of the river from the marsh field south side. It may go all the way across because the last third of the river-bed to the north had recovered itself with silt. It could have been the foundations of the small track from the mill into the mill-owned land as there was such shown on the Tythe map and Station Road was laid down very close to that point. Alternatively it could have been a fording track; and the river, before the Station Road bridge was constructed, could have been narrower, with the spit of land to the north now called The Avenue wider and without the stone wall it has had since the construction of Station Road. It is conceivable that the banks before that date of mid-nineteenth century were looser and fording of the river a more concurrent way to cross the river.

Moving up the line of the old route there can be seen just before the railway land, a very old brick arched bridge. Today it has under it the stream that follows the old route and the parish boundary into the river. It is now the access from Station Road into that field that was called great colly marsh.

Further up the old route turned sharply to the east around the fields to end up right at the homestead of Poundapit. Today's road was laid down to a straightened line and joined the newer main road to Cullompton, that junction is known today as Hele Cross. The old line as it turns to the east can be worked out from the field shapes as running close to two properties; at Lower Hillside or between that property and Riverhayes. There was, and to some degree still is, between the two properties a very large, wide thick hedge that must be centuries old. That could have been alongside the road. Beyond that the small water-course can be picked up again and most of it is on the line of the old road route up to Poundapit; past the front of the old farmhouse and on towards Clyst Hydon and Plymtree.

Following page: top illustration shows the old route across the river based on Surveyor's Drawings of 1796 (identifying names added); Below; part of the Deed Map of 1843 that shows the river at Hele. Next page: sketch of the hidden stonework on the river bed at Station Road bridge; photograph from road bridge when river low, in 2004 shows river bed stonework; sketch of arched bridge over the stream as it enters the field to the west of Station Road. On the third page: sketch map of the Broadclyst and Bradninch Tythe maps of 1841; Station Road added (coloured dark grey) to show the old and newer routes (identifying marks added to aid clarity).

Illustration based on the 1809 Devon Book of Maps, page 45, gives connected information.

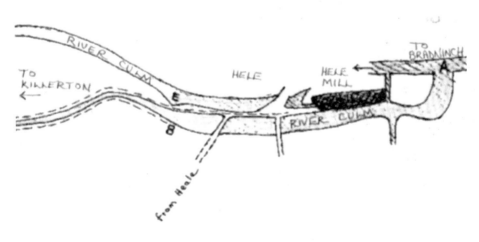

MARSH FIELD

RIVER BANK

RIVER CULM

THE PRYVE

MILL LEAT

MILL CAR PARK

Stoneway on river bed

gravel and Silt on river bed

to Hele Cross

STATION ROAD BRIDGE

to Hele Centre

MILL

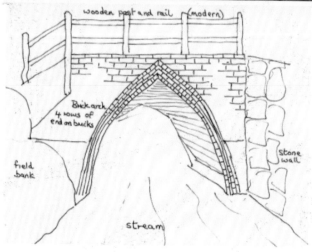

wooden post and rail (modern)

Brick arch 4 rows of end on bricks

field bank

stone wall

stream

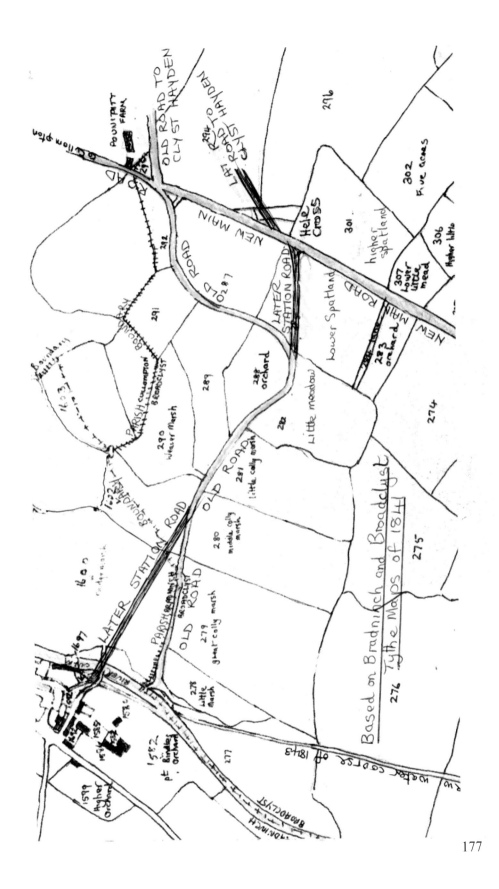

Based on Bradninch and Broadclyst Tythe Maps of 1844

THE PUZZLE OF LATE WARRENS LAND – IS IT REALLY RESOLVED.

I raised the problem of finding just small bits of information about the name of Warren in connection with the hamlet of Hele in my first book 'Memories from the Mill'. More research on WARREN – LATE WARREN – WALLENS – has produced results. History of Hele Mills brings in the name of Warren in the person of CHARLES WARREN in 1767. The name Warren appeared early in the history of Hele Mill. Charles Warren of Bradninch, who was a Paper-maker, leased that part of Hele Mills that was converted from Grist milling to Papermaking. That was from March 1767, from Abraham Elliot, who had earlier got a lease for all the Mill property at Hele, from an Edward Collins, when it was three grist (or flour) Mills. Edward Collins had got his lease from Francis Qwyn of Forde Abbey, and that works on backwards to the Royal ownership and Feudal system in England. Charles Warren continued with his lease of the Paper Mill until April 1770, when Abraham Elliot sold all interests of the Hele Mills to Mr.William Mathews and Mr.Thomas Dewdney and as these two men were papermakers they took over from Charles Warren.

Charles Warren leased the Mill for a short time, just three years. However he was classified on taking it over as 'of Bradninch, papermaker' so there were two possibilities; either a) he was working at or in charge of one of the paper mills at Kensham in Bradninch, and launched out on his own at Hele; or b) although from Bradninch was working at Hele and decided to have a go himself at running it. There are considerations as to the ending of his time at Hele. His lease was bought out by Thomas Dewdney in 1770 when Dewdney purchased the freehold of the Mill. Charles could have been given a 'price he couldn't refuse' for his lease or it could have been at the end of a short-term lease, or possibly he was failing at running the business and was giving it up. It is the sort of detail that would be lovely to know.

What is of interest to the puzzle of Late Warrens land in Hele is that Charles Warren, although he gave up the Papermaking Mill in Hele, seems to have then continued to own or lease substantial land and maybe the grist Mills and buildings around. It was certainly designated to his name and continued so down to the Tythe Map of 1841 although by then he had died. It leads one to consider that there was more going on in Hele at that time than Papermaking. The records talk of Dewdney taking over the papermaking from Charles Warren, they were of that craft, but there would have been the flour milling still continuing for some time and surely there was a homestead with that Mill and farming on the land around. The existence some seventy years later of areas of land right in at Hele identified as gardens and orchard on the Late Warrens land points to the possibility of a former homestead, even though by that time it had all been absorbed under the ownership of the family of Dewdney.

The map of 1840 following these notes shows the ownership with occupancy of the land and dwellings at Hele. Venmans was a homestead close in; also the Mill had its house right in the works area. John Dewdney didn't extend out from the Mill, except for two fields, although in the past it had been leased with good acreage.

178

The apportionment with the map tells us however he had ownership of all the buildings, even those that look as though they were outside the central Mill complex. That his brother, Robert Dewdney owned and occupied Heale Paine Farm (Hele Payne now) and Late Warren land and other fields encircling the Hele Mills, except for Venmans to the east, show there was a separation of land and property between the brothers according to their occupations.

To move on from Warren to the names, Wallens and Wallends. Those were the names used for the building at the lower end of Strathculm Road opposite the very old house on the corner. It was built as a row of stables, with hay lofts above, which opened onto what would have been a farm track leading from the hamlet to the nearby fields. Maybe it was linked to the Corner House if that had been the original homestead. That would have answered the question of where the original homestead was in Hele, with gardens and orchards and stables so close in to the centre.

The Mill must have bought or leased the building along with adjacent land and property at some time. The present, and the working name that the Mill calls that building are the very functional names 'The Sheds' or 'The Storage Sheds'. However the local name for it has come down from 'the Warren Sheds' to 'Wallens' and 'Wallends'. This means that they had been part of property of someone called Warren, and the only person found to be connected with Hele of that name was Charles Warren, Papermaker, from Bradninch of 1767.

Further information on this particular matter from people who gave their memories for my first book has opened out the interest. Firstly from Joan Carnell who is now in her eighties; Joan's late husband Cecil's father was called George. His wife, Joan's mother-in-law, had the maiden name of Warren. She came from Cullompton and Joan does not know if she was connected to the people named Warren that had been in Hele and in Bradninch. Joan knows there was also a family named Warren at the house at the junction of Budlake lane and the Killerton road near Killerton Chapel, but again does not know if they were connected to any other local Warren.

Cecil had a sister, and she married Albert Winney. Albert Winney is local-born and also like George Carnell, worked in the Mill at Hele. Albert is certain the buildings at the bottom of Strathculm Road were known as WARREN SHEDS. He remembers this from what he had been told by older people; that they were owned by a man called Warren who at the time lived in Bradninch. Albert also remembered in his own time that the building had been owned by a Mr.Warren in Bradninch who kept stores in it. Then individual people in Hele, connected to the Mill, used separate parts of it, one being Mr.Passmore from Ringmer House for logs etc. and so that had continued down to 1995 when the Hele Conservation Society took it over.

The mistaken use of the name WALLENS could have come about according to Joan in that there was a Lodge Man in the Mill, that she remembered, whose name was Mr.Walland and he did have one of the compartments for storage, in the Warren Sheds. And verbal reference in the twentieth century has continued to refer to the building as Wallens and Wallends.

Albert Winney, remembered that the Warren family in Bradninch had a shop in

Parsonage Street just onto the corner to Fore Street. He can remember as a child going by there and it had sweet machines outside to put a penny in and once on doing this all the sweets fell through so that was his lucky day!! It could have been a baker's or grocery store, but Joan is not absolutely certain on that. The first shop from there, in Fore Street, was a large Drapers and there was a Bakery behind there somewhere but the baker's shop may have been in Fore street also. Of some further interest, Joan's maiden name was Pook; her family came from Clyst Hydon originally even though she lived as a child in Upexe. Her father used to deliver flour from the grist-mill there both to the bakery in Hele and to the bakery at the bottom of Fore Street.

Further information from David Abrahams, who is now in his fifties, gives more insight. David has lived most of his life in Hele. He remembers from his mother, Ruby, that there was a Lodge Keeper of the Mill that was called Mr.Wallends, and that he had been the key-holder for the sheds in Strathculm Road. He had had one of the sheds for his own use, with other people who worked in the Mill using the others. Hence the local reference to them at that time that the building was Wallend's and anyone interested was sent to Mr. Wallend at the Mill Lodge. He used his section of the 'sheds' to store waste wood, which he chopped into firewood and sold to other Mill workers.

Also in the general knowledge of 'old Hele', David's mother was aware that the houses built as Hele Square in the middle of the nineteenth century had the ground floor rooms built of stone. They were the original one-storey farm buildings already there, and the walls were heightened with brick to create the two storey houses. That was all revealed when they were demolished in the 1970's, with one wall as such still in place running along the bottom of the garden of Rose Bungalow, David's home in Strathculm Road. It is a pity it is now behind a much newer block wall that the Mill built when they created a carpark on the land after the demolishment of the houses of Hele Square.

Hazel Rowlands who had lived in Hele Square in the early part of the twentieth century and who also recorded their demolition confirmed the structure of the houses in Hele Square.

Further information from Walter Wingrove who records his memories in a separate item in this book, page 49, had personal links to this matter in that he remembered as a Lodge-boy when he started at age 14, with a Mr. Miller as Lodge Keeper, he had the job of chopping up wood for firewood that was sold to workers. It would seem to have been a sideline of the Lodge Keeper over many years with different people in that position. The wood was most likely stored in 'Warren's' or 'Wallend's'.

To go back to much earlier references in Paper Mills in Devon – by A.H.Shorter Items nos. 41, 42, 43, Bradninch; Hele, Kensham, Paper Mills.
JOHN WARREN, paper-maker married in 1762. [no indication which paper-mill] also Colyton Parish records gives THOMAS WARREN, of Bradninch, paper-maker married in 1762. Presumably he married someone from Colyton in the Colyton parish Church. [no indication which paper-mill]
These small bits of information tell us that Warren was a name that was in the

Parish of Bradninch many centuries ago and, more importantly for the study of Hele, they were Paper-makers at the time when the reference to an owner of Hele Mills is the Charles Warren of 1767.

The Bradninch Parish records included the name of THOMAS WARREN as a Church Warden for St. Disen's, the Parish Church of Bradninch, in 1694, and also PETER WARREN as a Church Warden as above in 1713.

To come forward into the nineteenth century and the Census records of the parish of Bradninch we had some households with the name Warren. If they were linked from the earlier records it would be of satisfaction to have the family linked right through. On the Census of 1841 John Warren, aged 35, with wife Jane, aged 30 and children, John 12, Mary 8, Elizabeth 6, lived in Fore Street in Bradninch. He was a Schoolmaster. Also in the household Ann Warren aged 70, classified as a pauper, which meant she had no income and was most likely mother or close relative to John Warren. In a second household in Fore Street was Peter Warren, aged 30, with wife, Mary, aged 30, and children, William Ellis 6, Peter 3, John 2. Peter was a Shopkeeper.

In the next Census of 1851 John Warren, identified as born in Bradninch, his wife, Jane and Elizabeth, and a younger child, Walter 8, in the same dwelling in Fore Street. He was now a National Schoolmaster; Jane, was now a Schoolmistress.

In the second household in Fore Street Peter Warren, his wife, Mary, children Peter, John, and three younger, Elizabeth 9, Mary 7, Emily 1, were still living in their same house. He was now Assistant Overseer, his wife, Mary, was a Shopkeeper. A gravestone close to the Church records he died in 1870, Mary in 1888.

John Warren was aged 35 in 1841 so born in 1806; and Peter Warren, aged 30 so born in 1811. There is a gap to fill if they were descendants from the Charles Warren, Papermaker of Bradninch who worked the Hele Mill from 1767 to 1770. Ann Warren, aged 70 in 1841 goes the furthest back as she was born in 1771 and if descended from the Charles Warren could have been his daughter, daughter-in law, or granddaughter.

In 'Portrait of Bradninch' by Anthony Taylor, the owners of the large double fronted shop, no 49, at the bottom of Fore Street, was a Drapers shop on one side and Grocers on other side with owner as Peter Warren 1844-69; Peter Warren, his son, 1870-1908; Peter Warren, son of second Peter Warren 1909-23.

From more recent memories of people in the twentieth century the family of Warren had lived at No.14, Fore Street in Bradninch. One descendant of the family remembered that great grandfather had lived there. It is now called Hensleigh House, but it used to be called Warrens, although the older resident Mr.Warren didn't like that. He considered it too 'uppish' to have such a name for his house and so he still always referred to it as No. 14.

To finish in Hele, it seems that names continued down through the centuries long after the person involved had gone. Old documents leave clues, and memories change the context, so Warren, given the script writing of old could even have moved down in time from 'rr' to 'll' to Wallen; names lost but not now forgotten.

Previous information on the name Warren in my first book 'Memories from the Mill' – pages 141-145; 149-150.

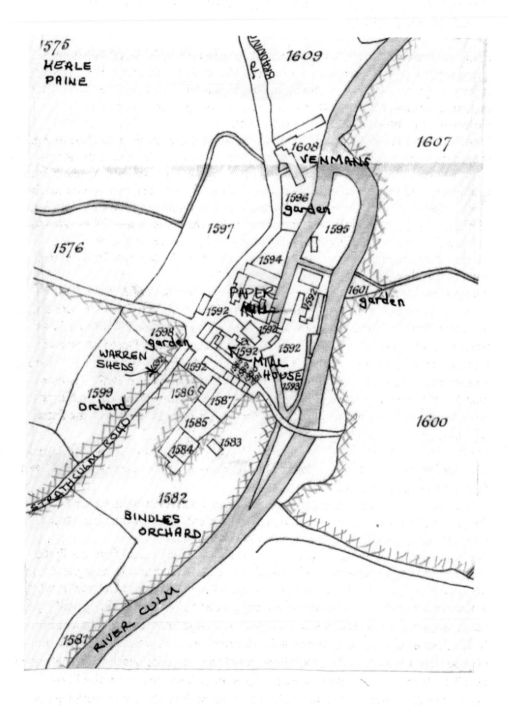

Illustration of a tracing taken in 1902 of the Tythe Map of 1841. The Original Tythe Map suffers from long usage and its paper surface is torn and faded in places. My copies in my first book gave as good as I could define it, but this 1902 copy is excellent of its original detail.

Identification names and the hatched boundary to show Late Warrens Land has been added.

182

THE PUZZLE OF BINDLES ORCHARD – THE SECOND FORGOTTEN NAME OF 'OLD HELE'.

In the very centre of Hele, within the land assigned to LATE WARRENS on the Tythe map of 1841 there was one area, no.1582, called 'part of Bindles Orchard'. It surrounded the central farm buildings in the hamlet. The name has never been explained or elaborated on either in records or from people's memories. However, new information has come to light.

Mrs Patricia Lovegrove, who is from Australia, visited Bradninch in 2003 and gave information she had gathered about her mother's family. The family name was Drew and of course to anyone interested in the important families from the past in Bradninch, and in the history of the paper mills, that name cropped up constantly. Mrs. Lovegrove could link the Drew family with two other well-known families, Mathews and Linnington, who were connected to the Mills in the eighteenth and nineteenth centuries. The Drew family were involved in ownership and management of various local paper mills. An item on the Martyn family in this book (page 135) linked in all those names.

Along with facts she gleaned from family vaults in the Parish Church which included 'John Earl of...Bodninch, died 23rd October A.D. 1624', there was a will of a John Drew of some 150 years later. That John Drew died 23rd March 1796 in Bradninch. He left to his wife, Elizabeth, 'messuages called Blackthorne and Blythwinds in Bradninch part and parcel of the Manor of Heale Payne'. There is an ancient barn and an area called Bithywinds today and named Bythawin on a map of 1889, which adjoined the land of Hele Payne Farm. The will continued with 'To son William messuages called Park in Bradninch'. Park was the farm adjoining the Kensham Paper Mills in the town.

In connection more specifically with Hele the important part of the will followed with 'and to his wife cottage, lanyard in Bradninch and Broadclyst, part of the Manor of Heale Payne called Bendalls'.

The arrival of the name Bendalls in that document was of interest. Heale Payne is the principal landed property of Hele; Hele is the only place where there was a short stretch of joint boundary between the two Parishes.

We have Bindles Orchard in the centre of Hele as already stated from the Tythe Map and in the Conveyance of Hele Mills in 1870. It is easiest to re-quote it from my first book (page 149). A section was conveyed named as Late Bindells; which at that time included 'said dwelling house, gardens plots Mill buildings cottages yards gardens 'and a second section 'that messuage known by the name of Bindles heretofore a part of the said Manor of Hele Payne.... together with nine cottages bakery and outbuildings erected on a piece ground formerly used as a Tan Yard .... is bounded by a certain road or lane leading to the River Culm'. Which proved that Hele Square had been built on the earlier buildings of Bendalls in the centre of Hele. As well as the cottages it listed a dwelling house but that dwelling was not identified. Also in the deeds a field made up of two orchards was under the name 'Late Bendells'.

Bendalls and Bindells are spelt slightly differently but they are similar and no other land name except Bindles is at all similar to either within the general area. The only meaning of the word 'lanyard' was as a nautical term, not a land term. Looking at old writing it seems possible and most probable that the word was 'tanyard' and the wife inherited a property, styled a cottage, and a tanyard in Hele. Bindles orchard enclosed the buildings in the centre, and at that earlier time it was a Tannery business. Abraham Elliot, a Tanner, sold the lease of three grist-mills at Hele in 1770 to Dewdney just as papermaking started. That date shortly pre-dates the Drew death and will of 1796. Elliot's Tanyard business would have pre-dated the papermaking and existed alongside the Mill in its early days of production of flour and then paper.

This information required further confirmation and a study of the 1841 Tythe map of the Broadclyst Parish. There it was found that at Hele, just across the wide marsh-land of the River Culm was an area of nine enclosures totalling twenty-two acres under the title of Bindles. The owner of the land was J.R.Sweetland, the occupier was John Salter. The field names were: Little meadow, two as Orchard, Five Acres, Copse close, Orchard close, Roundback, Higher little mead and Lower little mead. Most holdings of land had a dwelling attached but there was no dwelling or garden in that group; that would make sense if the cottage and one part of the land were in the hamlet of Hele, which was in the other parish adjoining it. In 1841, before the railway was laid through that area, the tracks and roads were different to those of today, but many of the positions and shapes of the enclosures remain the same. Item, Olden Hele, page 172, looks at the changes to the routes across the river and gives details of that area. Of interest when linking that land to its layout and its use today there is revealed a close connection of layout and usage. On those earlier fields and orchards of Bindles in the Broadclyst parish later stood until recently the Whiteways Cyder Works. It was surrounded by apple orchards; some of which are still there producing fine apple crops. Even in the small area 'part of Bindles Orchard' in Hele centre there are old apple trees, and many small pieces of land were listed as orchards on the old maps of Hele.

Another link in the chain was in the Hele Mill Visitors Book of 1912 (page 84) where one house name connects here. The Engineer's house was called 'The Bindles, Hele.' So the name did pass on down the centuries, but in this case gave no exact position of that property. However further facts follow in next item.

Above is a sketch of the front of the building 'Wallens' in Strathculm Road, as it is today.
Some information on 'Bindles' is in my first book 'Memories from the Mill' page 149

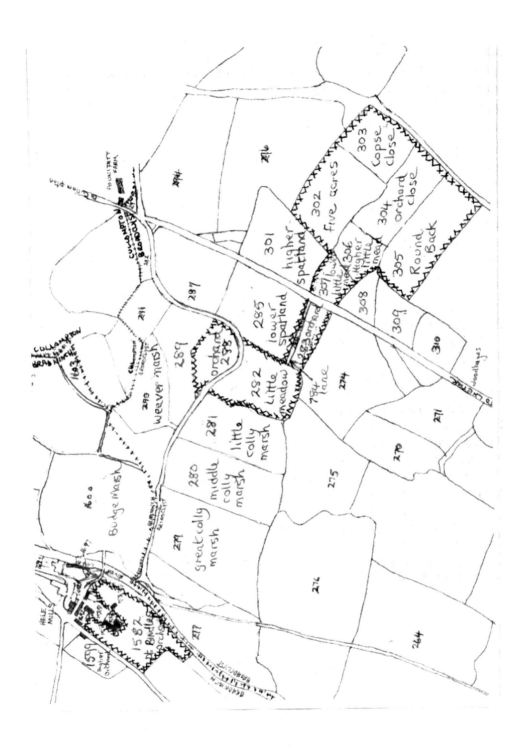

Illustration of the enclosures assigned to Bindles on the 1841 Broadclyst Tythe Map, and their proximity to Hele, the Mill, and enclosure of Bindle's orchard, on 1841 Bradninch Tythe Map. [Enclosures identified by hatched boundaries.]

THE PUZZLE OF AN OLD FARMHOUSE AT THE CENTRE OF HELE – IT STILL REMAINS UNDECIDED BUT MORE OF A POSSIBILITY.

Towards the end of my compilation of items for my first book 'Memories from the Mill' I became very interested in several 'puzzles' that surfaced. Two I have explored and the fresh findings precede this item. The third question I mentioned on page 157 as to whether or not the corner house, now known as Mews Cottage was the original homestead of the hamlet, with the other present-day houses along Station Road as the outbuildings and farm barns etc; or whether in fact the pair of houses -- 1, Station Road and 14, Hele Square -- were in fact the main homestead, with Mews Cottage a farm cottage and stables linked to it.
Exploration of the pair of houses reveals some secrets.
Historical records are few from before the mid-nineteenth century which was the time that the old farm settlement of the previous centuries was developed into an industrial village for the important workers of the Paper Mill; who then lived close under the buildings of their employment; the Paper Mill, at Hele. Their lives were entwined with living and work, and although the village was demolished in the 1970's, Hele Square is what remains in older minds as to what had always been there. But I have been thinking of the centuries before Hele Square.
Two houses were not demolished. They were the pair at the entrance to The Square, No.14, the Square and No.1 Station Road. I had assumed that they were small cottages, the same as the houses built up on farm yard buildings further in around the Square. This pair however, were structurally of larger and finer quality. The large main oblong of the property has 22 inch thick stone walls; the rooms are of a good height; the pitch of the roof steep as it obviously had been thatched in the past.
Ignoring the later additions of extensions at each end as kitchens, and outhouses and bedrooms and a complete dwelling, No.2 Station Road, at the back, the old main oblong reveals one house that was divided into the present-day pair. There would have been no windows except one on the landing maybe at the top of the main stairs on the back, north side; none on the east and west ends; all on the front side. The oldest entrance is the, 4 foot 6 inch, door into no.14, with the stone floor in that entrance hall right back to the back wall. All other ground floors in all the rooms are wood. The entrance hall has a strong old staircase up from it with panelling and carved handrail.
The rooms, two to the west of the hall and two (with a full length passage between) to the east all lie back to front in the house, all full width. There is a bricked-up door in the east wall of the hall, which means that all the rooms would have linked directly to each other, all doors opposite each other even when crossing the narrow passage in no.1.
That passage is an anomaly. It works now as it leads from the front door of no.1 to the back and to no.1's staircase; but that staircase has been constructed out of the back of one of the main rooms and is a squashed botched up affair. Without the stairs and when the building was one dwelling the narrow passage was purposeless. It could have been constructed using part of one of the two living rooms at the time

of conversion to two houses. If it had pre-existed that then a reason has to found. Now old longhouses in Devon did have that, it being a throughway from front to back, with the house on one side of it and animal shelter on the other side, all under the same roof. The choice is: the front of the farmstead was to the north with farmyard to the south; or the reverse. There is a bricked up door at the north end of the passage, but it is not possible to know what was outside at the rear. There is nothing shown on early records but No.1 was extended at the time of building Hele Square and later that was converted into a separate house which became No.2 Station Road. In the living-room abutting the back wall of No.1, there is within it the shape and wooden frame under plaster of that door.

Against that theory that the passage was the main entrance is that it is narrow and in longhouse design the through passage was functionally wide, and also only the side which was the house would have quality, but here the rooms both sides of the passage in No.1 are the same with fine quality woodwork. Both have large chimney places; one on the back north wall; the other on the end east wall. What does show is that the entrance into No.14, already mentioned is not only stone floored but also very wide and alongside the stairs it goes right back to the back. Also the rooms to the other, west side of that hall are different in that they have no quality picture-rails and woodwork.   So on that information it would seem that the dwelling had the principal entrance with stone floor at the door of no.14 with all house accommodation connected straight through the blocked-up door to the east. The possible pattern of living starts to be unravelled.

To continue the study in No.14 more fascinating features are revealed.   The hall area is now a concrete solid floor but over the old stone one and central and in front of the door is a 3 foot square of different concrete which is hollow underneath and under the door porch outside is also hollow. On the inner line of the external wall where the front door crosses there is a line of six holes, bolt or iron pipe diameter size, drilled through the present-day concrete; there is a depth of space below as a pole pushed down does not touch solid ground.   There could have been a cellar and the steps went down there from the central square of the hall.   Other possibilities were that it had been a well, or if that part of the building had been for animal shelter a gully and drain.   All three possibilities seem in unusual juxtaposition if in fact that was the main entrance to a large quality farmhouse. The two present-day rooms to the west of the hall are narrow with one chimney place only, on the end wall. Together they would be equivalent to the large rooms to the east already described. There is a newer inner wall at the back of the first room, part of which is a deep cupboard with wooden panelling at the back. The wooden floors here are a step up from the hall so I suspect that they have been put on top of an earlier solid, floor. The rooms, although having large old doors, have not the same quality in the woodwork, also no picture rails, instead there are wide wooden strips at the junction of walls and ceilings. The whole structure of both houses have walls and ceilings of lath and plaster with horsehair, some now centuries old and very fragile.

There could be a presumption towards the west, No.14, end being the working side of the farmhouse. As with No.1, you have to ignore the later addition of a kitchen and doorway through the thick external wall to it.   There is however a blocked up doorway in the north, back wall at the far end and it leads into the outbuildings, which was most likely a working area such as wash-house, scullery or dairy, and today a secondary staircase to the first floor. Again imagination has to be used as the pre-Hele Square development map showed a small block protruding there from the main 22 inch wall rectangle of the building. Around that back corner is a large square covered well. Those back stairs seem old but may have been added at the conversion to two houses except that it seems extravagant to have two stairways in a mill-worker's house. They could have been already there as external steps to above the outbuilding or into the first floor if it was at that time a farm storage space above animal accommodation.

To move upstairs the main layout, if we ignore the addition of a bathroom in no.14 and the creation of a bathroom in no.1, is of a wide passage along the whole length of the back, north wall. The main stairs come up in the centre from the ground floor entrance hall with the only window in the passage opposite the stairs. As with the ground floor bricked-up door in the wall east of the main door, the passage is built across just east of the top of the stairs; again at the dividing wall between the present two houses. The banister and panelling on the staircase continue to west and east right into that bricked up wall. When it was one dwelling all the bedrooms were along the whole length, each off that full-length passage. To start at the east, No.1, end, there was no staircase there (the present one is built as half of the width of the wide passage) and the present two narrow rooms would have been one large one over the living room below. The next room has been reduced to create the bathroom but would have been similar in size and depth. The Victorian corner fireplaces only start from the first floor and were added at the conversion. The original chimneys go up from below at east end wall and back wall.

A blocked-up door in the back, north, wall into the present-day No.2, Station Road, above the ground floor blocked-up door at the narrow through-passage, has not been resolved but it's possible that at conversion a small extension was added at the back and it was a back hall and stairs; then later to create No.2 Station Road, the narrow, cramped present stairway in No.1 was built from the back of the living-room downstairs up into the wide passage above, and the two doors blocked up.

In No.14 the bedrooms also led off the back passage to the front; the Victorian corner fireplaces, exactly the same as in No.1. The original chimney goes up from below at the west end wall. The bedrooms over the outhouses at the back do not seem part of the original layout but it is unresolved as to the links into the house in that area and at what time the outbuilding had a first floor added. Abutting the north wall in the long passage is a square chimney-stack passing up through; so some fire structure on the ground floor had been there. It doesn't show in the main house, unless a fireplace was behind the inner wall I mentioned earlier when describing the ground floor, otherwise it could have been from a wash-house in the outbuildings.

To move on to old records. There are many maps of the layout of houses after the creation of Hele Square with the conversion of that building to two houses in the mid-nineteenth century. The only earlier map of that dwelling that was of any size and clarity was the Tythe Map of 1841. An illustration of it (earlier item, page 182) shows the main rectangle (numbered 1587) as already studied above, with the small square outbuilding at the back (as of present day No.14). A small enclosure was directly from the west wall (present day garden and kitchen extension). The entrance to the farmyard, or Tannery, and orchards (named Bindles) seems to be in the position on the road the same as today's entrance to the car-park. That leaves the gardens in front of today's pair of houses the same area as in front of the original dwelling. An enclosure line went from the centre back to the west end of the very old cottage and stables (now called Mews Cottage) on the corner at the central junction of Hele.

That dwelling had a large entrance and the area in front of it was open to the side and front of the dwelling we are studying. What isn't there today is the row, with four of them individually identified, of buildings along the road. They must have been demolished when the road was straightened out to become Station Road. There was also no building at No.2 Station Road or barn link to Mews Cottage, so they were built after the 1841 Tythe Map time, most likely about the same time as the creation of the mill-workers houses of The Square. The Paper Mill used horses well into the twentieth century and with the farm buildings gone to provide houses for the workers there would have been a need for new stabling and fodder stores. That map could suggest a different aspect to the old structure of No.14 and No.1. If the main entrance was actually on the north wall, into the back to front passage of No.1 then it makes sense of that passage feature as the doors off of it are at the front, south, end. The large entrance through Mews Cottage also makes sense if it led to the front, entrance to the homestead. The 'back' oldest and largest chimney would then have been next to the main entrance which was often seen in old farmsteads as well as them often being on the end walls. Then the interconnecting doors from room to room would have led to the working stone hall with stairs up and domestic or animal shelter beyond. That scheme would make the front entrance into No.14 the external door to the farm etc. and could well have had cellars or a well under it. It is certainly another possibility.

Finally, to add interesting information, not of bricks and mortar, and not of old maps but of a different source in the twentieth century. This gives us a linking together of our puzzles of 'Olden Hele'. A house, as noted in the previous item on Bindles, was called 'The Bindles' Hele, in the 1912 Visitors book.(pages 183, 84) The tenant was P.Webster, Foreman Engineer but I could not identify the house although I could eliminate most properties in Hele through their house names. It still left some unnamed, including No.1 and No.14 and Mews Cottage.
Decoration instructions to Messrs. Nicks, builders in Bradninch, was given in 1946 by Wiggins Teape, owners of the Paper Mill and the houses in Hele. That was signed by Richardson the Manager at that time. The instruction was for 'Bindles, late Ewart's house'. The name had continued down a bit further! Mr.J.Ewart was the Engineer and retiring. The new Engineer coming was Mr. George Gall and he was the new tenant of the Engineer's house. The order gave the whole answer; first; 'Bindles' was described and it tallied only with No.14. That also supports the belief that the other side of the pair, No.1, had the name of ' The Laurels' on the 1912 Visitors book (page 84); home of another important employee,

J. Robertson Pierie, Foreman Papermaker.

The description of Bindles on the order had entrance hall staircase and landing, dining-room, sitting-room, kitchen, scullery, wash-house, two front bedrooms and sitting room upstairs and two back bedrooms; bathroom over kitchen, and back stairs.   With the written order very luckily was a sketch map of the rooms to save confusion on wallpapers and colours, and that corresponded exactly with No.14. An illustration of that sketch follows even though it is slightly confusing as it was a working sketch and draws first floor and ground floor on top of each other with a sitting-room upstairs above the end room which was the kitchen, and it labels rooms to the items of the instructions.   It has given us the information that was being looked for.   Bindles was the name of a dwelling, or even in older times, the Homestead at the centre of Hele.   It had been on the site of the pair of present-day houses No.1 and No.14 and had a farm, and possibly an important Tannery business, and orchards that were to become renowned for Cyder production.

To go right back to the first mention of a dwelling in Hele in 1796 (detailed on page 183) then called a cottage it would most likely have been the corner cottage, now Mews Cottage. That and the structure studied here were together the oldest dwellings in the centre of Hele; part of that farm with farm buildings and tannery. Close by on the other, northeast, side of the grist-mills was the ancient longhouse Venmans, (described in my first book, page 43) which had its land spread out in that direction but unfortunately it was demolished in the twentieth century as the Paper Mill expanded.   The other ancient dwelling was Hele Payne Manor, which was of major importance in the area.   It is now Hele Payne Farm and that is a couple of fields away to the north.   (These can be seen in juxtaposition on the illustration from the Tythe Map, 1841, page182).

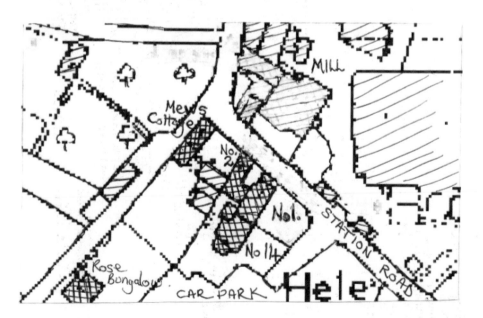

Illustrations. Above: Hele Centre today 2004. First two following pages : sketch plans of No.14 and No.1 showing the older features. Next: Map of nineteenth century Hele Square and Builder's sketch plan of 1946.

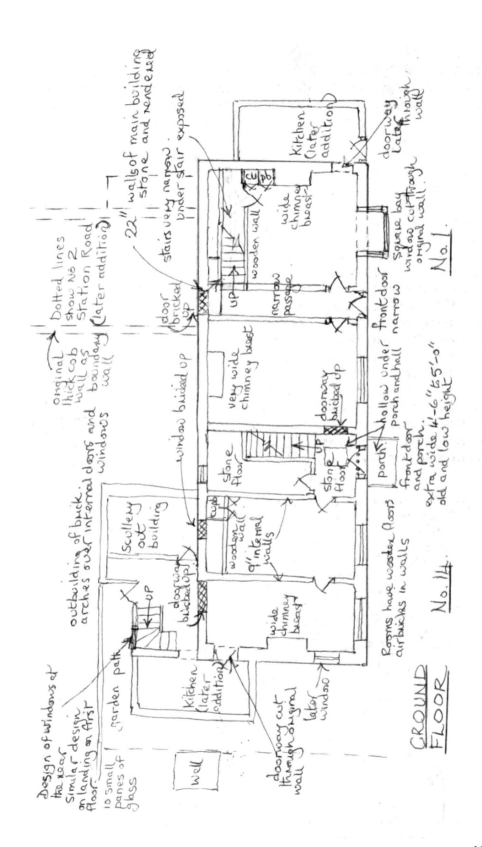

Design of windows at the rear similar design on landing an first floor

Dotted lines show No 2 Station Road (later addition)

10 small panes of glass

original thick cob wall as boundary wall

outbuilding of brick: arches over internal doors and windows

garden path

UP

Scullery out building

doorway bricked up

Kitchen (later addition)

wide chimney breast

doorway cut through original wall

later window

window bricked up

stone Floor

cupd
wooden wall
9" internal walls

stone floor

Rooms have wooden floors airbricks in walls

No.14

GROUND FLOOR

Wall

very wide chimney breast

UP

doorway bricked up

hollow under Porch and hall

Porch

front door and porch.
front door extra wide 4'-6" to 5'-0" old and low height

22" wall of main building stone and rendered

door bricked up

stairs very narrow under stair exposed

UP

wooden wall

narrow passage

cu
pb

wide chimney breast

square bay window cut through original wall.

narrow front door

Kitchen (later addition)

doorway later through wall

No. 1

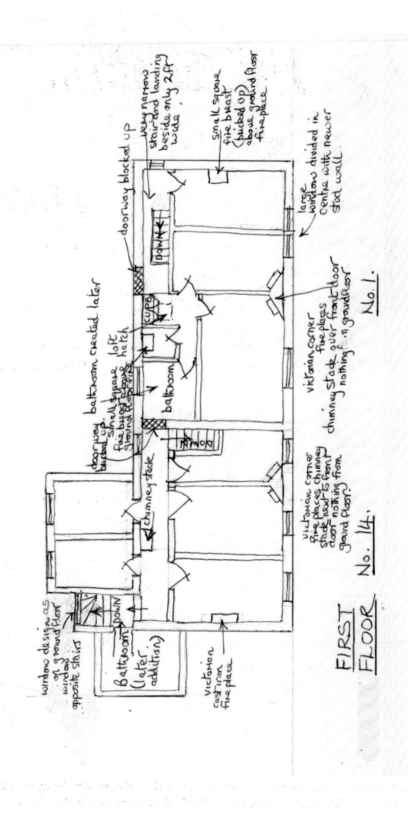

FIRST FLOOR

No. 14.

No. 1.

window design as on ground floor ... window opposite stairs

Bathroom DOWN (later addition)

Victorian cast iron fire place

chimney stack

doorway blocked up. Small square fire breast above ground floor fireplace

bathroom created later

loft hatch

CUPB

bathroom

DOWN

victorian corner fire places chimney stack next to front door nothing from ground floor.

victorian corner fire places chimney stack over front door nothing in ground floor

very narrow stair and landing beside only 2ft wide.

doorway blocked up

DOWN

Small square fire breast (bucked up) above ground floor fire place

large window divided in centre with newer stud wall

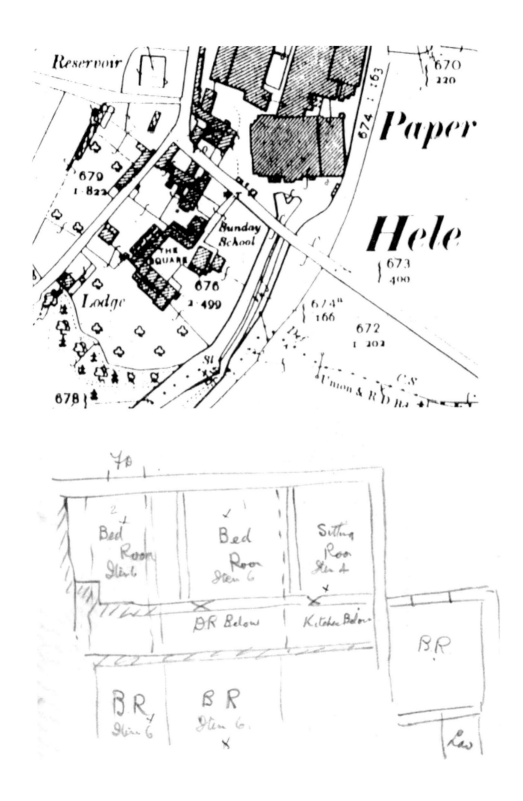

Top illustration: Mid Nineteenth Century map of Hele after the development of the old farmstead into Hele Square.   Below: Builder's sketch plan of 'Bindles', 1946.

Conclusion – by Paddy Nash
HELE TODAY IN THE YEAR 2005.

I have reached the year 2005 at Hele. How more complex, intertwined and varied are the lives of the people who have been here or worked here than I had thought ten years ago. More hidden or forgotten or ignored items of historical interest have been unearthed and come to light. As with the beginning of the interest to compile these two collections I had to go to the Paper Mill so I end there.

The peak of industrial papermaking was in the early to mid nineteenth century and the Culm River supported up to seven or more of such mills, which was one of the largest groups within England. In the mid twentieth century Hele Mill under Wiggins Teape Ltd. was part of a large paper production company with a Head Office for all the commercial organization and production of paper at Mills across the country. In the decades after them new owners of Hele Mill created many developments on the business side at Hele.

One thing of great significance a decade ago, at a time of difficult market forces, was the positive decision by Bibby, the owners, to create a new paper machine. It was designed and installed at Hele and became PM5 – the fifth paper machine at Hele Mill in its industrial history. Difficulties, commercial and functional, prevented the machine producing the breakthrough for success that was required of it and it was 'mothballed' for a time.

Seeing Silverton Mill close down its papermaking at the turn of the century and become a general industrial site, one wondered how long the two remaining Paper Mills, at Hele and at Cullompton, along the River Culm would last. It was with trepidation that we who lived in Hele watched 'our' Paper Mill go through a rather low time. Changes of ownership (some maybe for commercial usage rather than for skilled paper production) has hopefully now ended; we are optimistic with its purchase by a long established British paper makers, R.J. Crompton.

We have lost the fine specialised paper production of the past such as banknote paper, quality writing paper and industrial filter papers, and although now into different product papers they are still producing fine specialized papers, concentrating on those required for the food industry. Crompton has got the PM5 back into production. Hele Mill has survived changes over the centuries, both locally and from international monetary changes and world-wide events.

The creation of the PM5, in a new machine-house of 10,000square metres, aimed to combine speed of production with maintenance of correct quality of the product. Any future research and recording the memories of the workers in the Paper Mill should be about the skills of the individual tasks in papermaking; not only in the past but of those of today.

On the following page is a photograph of the new driers for PM5 arriving across the River Culm at Hele. The driers were just one small part of the papermaking machine.

That page and this book are completed by two impressions of that event. The middle illustration is by Jack Nash, aged 9; the bottom one by Emily Nash, aged 6.

194

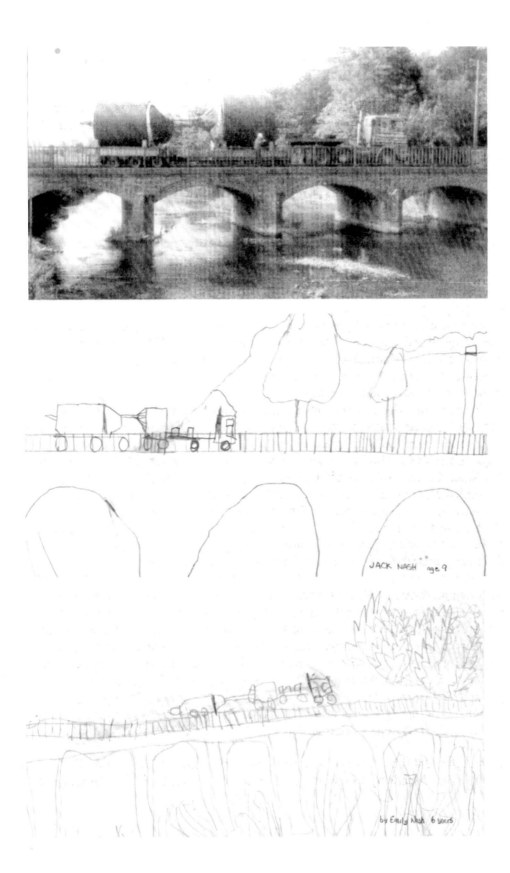

JACK NASH age 9

by Emily Nash 6 years

NOTES FOR THE READER………….

Correction of Editor's mistake: Page 31 line 17: Lilly Slater's maiden name was Hales;
line 41: The Paper Mill was Silverton not Hele.